The Magic Doorway into the Divine

✦CONTACT US✦

To order additional or multiple copies or to be added
to our secured mailing list to receive notices of forth-
coming CD's and books, please visit our website at:
www.themagicdoorway.com

To arrange a speaking engagement or to enquire about
arranging a private telephone consultation,
please e-mail your request to:
devrahlaval@telus.net
and leave a message with your contact information.

The Magic Doorway into the Divine

Devrah Laval

Mystic Lights Publishing

Vancouver, British Columbia, Canada

Note for Librarians: A cataloguing record for this book is available from Library and Archives Canada at www.collectionscanada.ca/amicus/index-e.html

      Canadian Cataloging in Publication Data
      Laval Devrah
      The Magic Doorway into the Divine
      ISBN: 978-0-9784986-0-3

1. Spirituality 2. Mysticism 3. Religion 4. Self-Help 5. Philosophy

PERMISSION CREDITS
The author and publisher would like to thank the following for granting permission to use material in this book:
SYDA Foundation for material featuring
Gurumayi Chidvilasananda, Swami Muktananda, and Swami Anantananda.
Element Books, Inc. for material featuring Rajinder Singh.
Sawan Kirpal Publications for material featuring Darshan Singh.
Oneworld Publications for passages from *Mysticism* by Evelyn Underhill.
Every effort was made to locate the copyright holders of copyrighted material contained herein. In the case of inadvertent omission, please contact the publisher.

      Edited by Donaleen Saul
      Cover Photograph: J. P. Stevan
      Cover and Interior Design: Kiskis Designs
      PRINTED AND BOUND IN CANADA

Mystic Lights Publishing
West 4th Avenue RPO
P.O. Box 19173
Vancouver, B.C., Canada V6K 4R8
jpstevan@telus.net
www.themagicdoorway.com

10 9 8 7 6 5

✤DEDICATION✤

*To all of my great teachers who draw from
the same Immaculate Source
where there is no name and no form,
just limitless Light and Love...*

✤What is this Doorway?✤

What is this doorway?
And does someone hold the key?
When can I come through?
Who can set me free?
I punch, I scream, I kick the door
And still I cannot see.
I'll fight: I'll kill until the end
To have my victory.
The years have gone: my youth has died,
But not my misery.
There must be more that I can do.
I cannot simply 'be'.
No longer can I fight, no longer can I kill.
Who is this enemy?
Just then the door has opened wide
And all I see is me.

Contents

Part Four – The Journey Beyond the Doors

Part Five – Returning to the Garden

✤FOREWORD✤

In the Upanishads, Sankara, the great Advaitin scholar, characterizes the process by which one comes to know the Self as follows: "That which is devoid of all duality is described by adhyaropa and apavada, i.e. by super-imposition and negation, by attribution and denial."

This book is about that paradoxical process of freeing the Self from all forms of attachment, suffering, and spiritual temptations only to discover, in that final phase of illumination, that the Self was never separate from God. There was no real duality to be overcome. This is the conclusion in the most famous instruction on the Self in the Chandogypa – Upanishad in chapter 9, verse 4: "Tat tvam asi, That Thou Art."

But it would be a trap of the spiritual ego to simply know this with the mind; one must go through all of the stages of awakening and purification passionately, with one's whole being.

Devrah's book is a powerful application of this princi-ple, for it has been birthed from the depths of her being. It has emerged from the burning crucible of her life so that the realization of non-duality is the Truth she inhabits moment by moment.

Rarely has a soul written of these classic stages of the mystical path with such candidness, creativity, and courage. Her "Door Openers" and "Door Closers," which describe how the same experience can either open us to God or close us off, depending on our relationship to it, are unique.

But when Devrah describes her Dark Night of the Soul, you feel utterly drawn into the immensity of her heart and thus of God's Heart. For Devrah's book is a passionate account of a lover of God who finally realizes that this whole journey is about Love. It is about God's Love that has been seeking us since the beginning of time. In the Catholic Mass, there is a phrase, "Quarens me sedisti lassus," which translates as "Faint and weary Thou haste sought me." The great Jewish mystic, Simone Weil, interprets this to mean it is God seeking us out; not the other way around as is commonly believed.

Devrah's fearless account of her own journey reminds us that we are both the subject and the object of our longing.

Shirley Anne McMurtry, Ph.D.

✤PREFACE✤

The vision for *The Magic Doorway into the Divine* came to me while walking along a country road one hot summer's day in the mid-1990's. It was to be a simple book filled with poetry, meditations, and conversations with God. A couple of years later, I met an East Indian mystic who, upon meeting me for the first time, said, "You must write that book, it will help a lot of people." I was startled that he would know a secret that I had forgotten; but I was also inspired to begin scratching down a few notes. In the process, a larger force began to take over, and eventually my scribbles blossomed into this book.

The Magic Doorway into the Divine chronicles a search that began 25 years ago when a life-altering mystical experience and profound healing awakened me to my true Self. The effect of this awakening changed my life so completely that everything I had assumed to be true evaporated, leaving me in unknown territory. For many years I walked through a fire that opened my heart, seared my soul, and graced me with the knowledge that we are not just small, limited creatures. We are one with God's love.

Like a phoenix, *The Magic Doorway into the Divine* arose out of the ashes of this fire. In the writing, it taught me about the power of Divine Love and how such Love can be found in every moment of life, with every person, in every place, and in every thing. The metaphor of the magic doorway is an image to help us understand what opens the doors, what closes the doors, and what takes us beyond all doors to the Garden of Love.

Spirituality is romanticized by many seekers who do not fully understand or do not wish to acknowledge that the pain one can experience in letting go of the ego can be horrific at times. In this book, I share some of my experiences and hold nothing back about the suffering as well as the joy that I have encountered in this journey to Truth. Enlightenment is not a linear process and cannot be controlled or captured with the mind. I have learned that one must embrace contradiction as an essential part of the journey.

Each section of *The Magic Doorway into the Divine* begins with a conversation between God and a Being of Light from a faraway galaxy. Their discussion about a lesson that human souls on Earth need to experience is followed by a poem that takes the reader more deeply into the heart of the matter. The teachings are then expanded upon by a philosophical essay, followed by short self-help "meditation keys" that can open the door into the reader's own divinity.

Part I, Crossing the Threshold, expresses the miraculous power and healing that is possible when we touch the Truth.

Part II, The Door Openers, is a celebration of what we can be when we turn our minds to a higher perspective and, like alchemists, transmute every situation into love.

In Part III, The Door Closers, the poetry is written from

the perspective of the ego, which has no interest in God or divinity. These poems are intentionally provocative in order to help us see our delusions more clearly.

Part IV, The Journey Beyond the Doors, takes us into The Dark Night of the Soul, where nothing undertaken from the perspective of the personal will works. We discover that all mind-focusing concepts and techniques that might have worked in the past, no longer do. Any spiritual technique employed to open the doors to our higher being has no power. We also find that we are unable to control our lives as we once thought we could; whoever we have believed ourselves to be has been "erased." This purification of the ego can be very distressing, but its ultimate goal is to take us to true humility. This, then, is where we learn that all striving is useless; not a breath do we take without the Grace of God. There is nothing left to do but to surrender to God's will.

In Part V, Returning To The Garden, we are new again, like chicks emerging from the cosmic egg, seeing the world with brand new eyes, seeing beauty and love in everything, accepting ourselves, letting go of the inner and outer war, and returning to the true Source.

The Magic Doorway into the Divine helps us to take our life challenges – personal, financial, and other types of losses; relationship issues; physical, mental, and emotional health concerns; spiritual emergencies, etc. – to a new level of consciousness. It teaches us how to bring unconditional love to every part of life, something that all of us, regardless of age, race or culture, long to experience. This book encourages us to take responsibility for our lives and to actively participate in our healing transformation. There is nothing wrong with anything that we undergo in life. Everything is a magic doorway to God's love.

Devrah Laval

xvi

✤Acknowledgments✤

I wish to acknowledge all of the great teachers and masters who have come into my life. I am especially thankful for my family, friends, relationships, and acquaintances who have taught me about Love, in its many forms.

I also wish to thank Donaleen Saul and Julius Kiskis for their love, patience, and expertise as they helped me put this book together; David Pacula for his wonderful research; and J. P. Stevan whose infinite love and support allowed me to birth this book.

Also, deep gratitude to the girls in my group who have stuck with me for fifteen years: Glynis, Laura, Cara, Carol, Michelle, Anne Marie, Juliette, and Leslie.

Thank you to my friends who have given their continued support while writing this book: Trixie, Shanti, Mandakini Rene, Bernard, Teja, Eckhart, Pauline, Suman, Paddy, Iala, Anne McMurtry, Krystal, Lili, Lynn, Kosto, Dhorea, Carey. I would also like to acknowledge my brothers Michael and David, and my mum and dad. And to anyone else, whom I might have missed, thank you.

A percentage of the profits from the sale of this book are donated to organizations that are committed to the physical and spiritual upliftment of humanity.

*Magic is the recognition of the ordinary
becoming extraordinary.*

✦INTRODUCTION✦

There is a secret doorway to our Divine Self that is simple, obvious, and available to us in every moment. We do not need to run away from the world of people and problems; we can fully enter into this world and receive the gifts that each situation presents.

When I was younger, I neither welcomed life's challenges nor enjoyed interactions with people. I felt that such ordinary engagement with life would interfere with my connection to my inner Self and preferred to live in a state of separation. I considered day-to-day trials and responsibilities to be boring and just wanted to be free.

As I matured, I saw that all of these "boring" trials were actually doorways that could take me deeper into my God Self. I also learned that it is difficult to enter these doorways when we believe only the surface experiences of boredom, pain, frustration, and other passing states of mind. Believing such states to be the only reality leaves us without love, peace, or joy. There comes a time when we become so tired of the empty repetitiveness of the surface reality that we long to find the key that will open each door and allow us to return to *who we really are* – beyond our personalities, concepts, and facades.

What then is this key? I have discovered that it is an alchemical fusion of two elements. The first is love and acceptance of our present state, however bored, sad or frustrated we might be. The second is our sincere intention to know the truth of *who we really are*. This magic key forged from self-acceptance and a sincere desire for the truth can transform ordinary vision into extraordinary vision. It can help change our perspective so we see life anew. With the help of the magic key, our "boring" everyday life becomes a gift from the Creator, and our "limited" partner becomes a god or goddess. The magic key helps us realize that we don't operatè alone. The love of God permeates every particle of the Universe; all aspects of our life, relationships and reality are an expression of that Love.

It is only with the magic key of love and acceptance of what is that we can be freed of the boxes, labels, and judgments that have been imposed upon us and have limited our true potential. When we learn to accept all aspects of ourselves as God, then separation dissolves and wholeness reigns supreme.

In her video, *Living, Loving and Aids*, Elizabeth Kubler Ross spoke of the scientific community wanting to use children born with AIDS as guinea pigs for research into the disease. Dr. Ross considered such intrusions to be a violation, and instead adopted some of the babies and offered them unconditional love and one-on-one bonding. This love had such a profound effect that some of the babies were able to develop their own antibodies. According to Dr. Ross, if the babies were cared for, cuddled and loved, "They just blossom(ed) like a flower."

We may not always be held or cuddled like Dr. Ross's AIDS babies, but if we show ourselves and others the same compassion, and if we uphold a wholehearted intention to know a higher Truth, then a presence of Love does begin to surround us and hold us.

Masters like Jesus lived in the open doorway of divinity, and through the power of unconditional love they could look at or touch people and heal them completely. Their conviction penetrated all the labels and beliefs surrounding these individuals, exposing their inherent perfection. Jesus would often entertain thieves, prostitutes and others who were seen as the dregs of society because He had no judgment toward any of God's creatures. He responded to each person with absolute love and requested that everyone strive to do as He did:

> "But I say unto you, Love your enemies and pray
> for those who persecute you, so that you may
> be sons of your Father who is in heaven; for he
> makes his sun rise on the evil and on the good,
> and sends rain on the just and on the unjust.
> For if you love those who love you, what reward
> have you? Do not even the tax collectors do the
> same? And if you salute only your brethren,
> what more are you doing than others? Do not
> even the Gentiles do the same? You, therefore,
> must be perfect, as your heavenly Father is
> perfect." [1]

But rather than having the "perfect" perception that transcends the labels, we've learned to judge ourselves and others according to assertions of right or wrong, good or bad, or according to dictums as to what is God and what is not God. Such judgments only distance us from the love we crave from the depths of our soul. To embrace the whole is to live from a place where nothing else exists but God. Every moment of our lives is another opportunity to drink the nectar of God's Grace, not only in our churches, ashrams or temples, but everywhere, always – with everyone and everything we encounter. Then, with the eyes to see the Truth, our life and everything in it becomes a magic doorway to divinity and a temple to our own God Self.

I invite you to open your hearts and minds, to journey with me in the discoveries I've made from the many lessons and teachings with which I have been graced. These took me along many pathways, detours and bridges that ultimately brought me to the understanding that nothing exists but God's unconditional Love.

The Journey

A stream of grace seduces me into itself.
The light is so bright, yet so gentle.
It cradles me like a child -
Healing me, and giving me Love like I've never known.
As I grow comfortable wading here,
The seasons change. The waters rise.
And the stream becomes a flowing river.

The river is passionate, like a lover
And it enters every orifice and satiates every desire,
More than any earthly man could.
What more do I need?
I have everything here!
So I dive in, trusting the flow of the river.

The seasons change
And the river grows more intense.
Its raging waters deposit me into a furious ocean.
I thrash around, struggling for life, gasping for breath,
Abandoned and betrayed by the light.
Darkness is all around me now - no light to be found.

I keep trying to escape,
But all I meet is fear, anger, helplessness, and pride.
I grow so tired. My heart is broken,
Shattered to the core.
Death would be a welcome relief.

But I am suspended in this deep, dark ocean
Waiting for what, I do not know.
Exhausted and beaten, I finally give up the fight.
I am ready to die. I have nothing left to hang on to.

I fall into the dark stillness I have always feared.
I face it. Breathe it. I rest in it, and I become it.
The ocean that was swallowing me becomes me.

The tides change.
I am washed up on the shore,
But strangely I am the shore too.
I am the bird that sings,
The pebbles that shine in the sun.
I am even the sun.
"Where did I go?" I wonder.
Now I know.
My small I has been replaced by everything.

Part

1

Crossing
The Threshold

Once upon a time, a Being of Light from a far away galaxy looked down upon Earth and asked God, "Why do they suffer? Why do they forget? Aren't we all free?"

God replied, "Yes, but sometimes a soul needs to forget for a while in order to find the doorway back to divinity".

"But why this game?"

"To know love in the human heart is the greatest game of all. To be reunited in the place of greatest separation is the highest service to all of Creation. The human body contains within it a precious jewel hidden in the heart. The longing of the soul creates the seeking and eventually the finding of the unsurpassable joy of knowledge. Humans have a body in order to know attachment, separation, emotion, sensation, insecurity, fear, darkness, light, confusion, clarity, living, dying, greed, hate, love, pride, humility, lust, self-righteous-ness... All of these experiences pull the heart apart, until one day when the pain is too much and a little prayer is uttered, the light seeps through the cracks and human beings fall to their knees, humbled before me, forgiven, embraced, renewed, and made whole. We separate so we can play this game, so we can experience my great Love that exists in every way and in every thing. Humans are my most precious children and so we play hide and seek. I am never far away. I am just hiding behind the Magic Doorway, waiting to shower them with the brilliant light of their own eternal Self."

The Awakening

I guess it was my time or rather God's time. I was 29 years old, I had a good husband, I was a successful model and dancer. By conventional standards, I had an enviable life, and yet I felt somehow empty. Something was haunting me.

Then, during a routine check-up, my doctor told me that my uterus had completely dissolved and I would never menstruate again. I would never have any children. I was devastated by the news and was telling a friend about it when she told me about an upcoming workshop designed to take participants to enlightenment [2] provided they were willing to apply themselves. I felt a surging force of desire, stronger than anything I had ever known. My simple response to her was, "I must go!"

We both forgot about my uterus.

Getting myself to the workshop was surprisingly difficult. When I told Jeff, my husband, he said, "You can't go." He had never tried to prevent me from doing anything before, but this time he was not only adamant but angry. I felt that I was fighting for my life. I told him I was going anyway. The next day, I asked my boss if I could take Saturday off but he refused. Like my husband, he was adamant. I told him I was sorry but I must go. By the time I left for the weekend, I had no idea if I would have a job or a marriage when I returned on Monday. But I felt as if something greater was driving me and I had no control over it.

Sleeping bag in hand, I was dropped off at an old monks' retreat/lodge outside the city. Everything was white and austere. No flowers. No colour. There was one tiny closet for everyone's clothes. Each small bedroom had eight hard bunk beds. It was an icy cold night in November and everything felt harsh, cold, and naked. I just wanted to go home, but I also knew I had already crossed the line and there was no returning. I was ushered downstairs to the workshop room with the other participants where we were welcomed with herbal tea and honey. All of our valuables were collected, packaged, and stored away for safekeeping. We were not allowed to wear watches, jewelry, makeup, or cologne; nor were we allowed to drink coffee or eat anything other than the macrobiotic food provided.

We were told that during the workshop we would be paired off and would face our partners for one-hour intervals in which we would take turns asking each other one question, "Tell me who you are." We would have an uninterrupted period of time to answer and then we'd switch roles. After an hour of this, we'd change partners and continue again. This would go on for 18 hours each day apart from rest and meal breaks.

On the first night, we did a few exercises to prepare ourselves, to get to know one another and to learn the technique. At the end of the evening, we collapsed into our hard, cold bunk beds. Nobody slept. We were awakened at 5:00 AM. It was horribly cold, I got up, stumbled to the bathroom, and made my way to the workshop room where I sat across from a half-asleep stranger who asked me the question, "Tell me who you are."

I was miserable. I am not a morning person and have a great aversion to talking to anyone without at least a cup of tea first. But then breakfast arrived, I got a chance to shower, and returned to the routine. The sun slowly began to shine through and I began to feel better. Even my partners became more interesting and alive as they too began to warm to the routine. Alternating every few minutes, we continued asking each other the question, "Tell me who you are."

I enjoyed baring my soul in this very safe environment. However, the facilitator warned us: "Stay focused on experiencing and communicating the absolute truth of, 'Who you really are.'" Hours went by, lunch came and went, more cleaning, more exercises. The room began to take on a palpable quality of other worldliness. It was surreal. Day turned to night and I was exhausted. My head began to ache but I had to keep going. "Who am I?" "Who am I?" Over and over again. "Who am I?" became my mantra. By bedtime I was so sick and exhausted, I thought I would die.

I fell into the bunk bed and slept a bit. Then at 5:00 AM the morning bell rang, announcing the beginning of Day Two. I couldn't believe that we could be so tortured. To the bathroom and then down to the workshop room to sit in front of another partner with bad breath asking me, "Tell me who you are."

I was getting angry and the pain in my head was getting worse. I thought of running away but there was no transportation back to the city. Breakfast passed, showering, more partner work, lunch. The pain and frustration was getting worse for all of us. Many had vomit bags next to them. The pain in my head was unbearable; I felt as though it was about to explode. Finally, at about 4:00 PM, every cell in my body felt like it was being crushed. I couldn't bear it anymore. My partner asked the question, "Tell me who you are."

I looked him straight in the eye and said with the most rage I had ever expressed in my life, "Who the Hell do you think I am!?!" Then with great force, I screamed out, "I Am Me!" At that moment, I heard a huge cracking sound at the top of my head. Suddenly, I was free of all of my aches, pains, and limitations. Perhaps this is how death feels.

I became a very large presence. The facilitator noticed and came rushing over, saying, "Who are you?" I replied, "I Am Me!" I couldn't describe in words this all-pervasive experience of freedom and knowing, but the "Me" I felt was not my body or personality. "I am God!" I said. Then I pointed to myself and said, "This is God." "I Am!" The facilitator laughed heartily.I began to laugh uncontrollably and fell off my chair. I rolled around on the floor in fits of ecstasy, laughing at all of the lifelong beliefs that I was just this body and its desires, hopes, and dreams. I wanted to share my joy with some of my other partners but they just sat there looking at me as if I was insane. They remained in the same great misery that I had just come out of. I realized in that moment that I was having a deep inner experience, not anything visible except for the light that some could see emanating from my body that divine day.

For the rest of that day and night I was bathed in light and felt love toward everyone and everything. All the things that I had hated the day before were now luminous and beautiful. I spent three hours weeping as I looked at my hand and arm. I was awestruck at the miracle of the body that I lived in. I felt great reverence for the power that lay behind this magnificent creation, even though I now knew that I was that power. I was experiencing the divine union of my body and soul. Nothing has ever come close to the supreme joy of that state. Every person who sat before me was God. And by the end of the weekend, I knew that I would never be the same again.

When I arrived home, my husband was happy to see me and I still had a job on Monday - at least for a while. Each person I interacted with at work felt divine. Looking deeply into their eyes, I felt tremendous compassion for them as they shared their problems with me. I knew then that God knows everything about us and has infinite patience.

But the most unexpected and shocking change was that I began to menstruate after not having been able to for five years. My doctor was curious and concerned and ordered some tests. A few days later, he called and told me that my uterus was completely whole and perfectly healthy. A specialist in his field, the poor man was baffled. But I knew that a miracle had taken place.

Free at Last

The dark cloud bursts

And I emerge as the blue sky -

Pure

Limitless

And free

With a joy that surpasses all earthly joys

I have ever known.

Returning To
The World

After my awakening experience, I lived in a state of great light and bliss for about a year. Then, the light began to fade and my life seemed much more difficult. During that challenging time when the darkness seemed so overwhelming, something deep within continued to haunt me, never letting me forget *who I really am.*

Soon after my awakening experience, my marriage ended and fame and fortune began to pursue me. I was just an aerobics teacher/dancer and model, but during this phase, people were drawn to me like bees to honey. In the early 1980s, my picture was on the front page of a major Canadian newspaper with an accompanying full-page article declaring me a "Goddess Revolutionizing Fitness." Shortly thereafter, I was offered a morning spot on Canada AM. Other Canadian and American television producers were calling, wanting to offer me my own health and fitness show, or appearances on other shows already on the air. A well-known soft drink company offered me a lucrative contract to be an international fitness spokesperson for their product. Movie offers and modeling contracts appeared. Perhaps they were drawn by the energy of my awakening experience, but people in positions of power wanted to turn me into a star. My friends were awestruck at all that was coming my way. It was overwhelming. I was being picked up in limousines, meeting with celebrities, and "taking" meetings to discuss impressive-sounding business deals. The world and all of its glory rushed towards me, and every dream and fantasy I had ever had appeared at my doorstep. This was the worldly face of my awakening. However, the new energy cascading through my body would not allow itself to be controlled; I could not be coerced into becoming a Hollywood persona.

I had had such a profound transformation in body and psyche that integrating the new hormones and energies was difficult. I found myself shaking a lot because of the kundalini energy traveling up my spine. With the sudden appearance of a uterus, my hormones were in turmoil. My body was trying to balance itself, a natural process but very uncomfortable. All I wanted to do was to run away from the chaos, inner and outer. I went on retreat to contemplate all that was taking place and came to realize that I could neither control what came my way nor what might leave me. When I returned, the

promised fame and fortune began to dwindle and soon
dissolved. I was living in such bliss that the loss of fame
and fortune did not trouble me. Other experiences
took precedence. I became highly sensitive to other
people's thoughts and feelings, and discovered that I
had healing and psychic powers. People would share
stories of being healed of an illness or having experienced some kind of awakening after speaking with me
or taking one of my classes. I was living almost continually in a state much larger than my personality, but I did-
n't fully understand what I was feeling and experiencing. It was as if I was my Soul rather than my personality. Not having a guide or mentor to provide context or
to mirror my state, I was greatly confused as I struggled
to continue to live my life in the old way. This confusion
was compounded by the energies that were moving
through my body. Sometimes they took the form of tor-
rential sexual energy. Sometimes I experienced intense
irritation and psychic sensitivities that made it difficult
to be with other people for very long because I would
feel their unexpressed feelings in my own body. I could
no longer stand noise or crowds; I craved nature, peace
and quiet, and a more meditative lifestyle.

My relationships with some of my friends and acquaintances changed, as I could no longer drink wine, go to
parties, watch TV or movies, or even drink coffee. All of
these former pleasures made me feel ill. My new body
demanded a life of purity that eliminated those friends
who could neither understand nor accept that I was no
longer "fun" in the old way. I even lost a boyfriend who
was dear to me. My work life changed as well. I broke
my foot, which prevented me from doing my fitness
classes or dance work for a number of months. People

began gravitating to me seeking spiritual workshops, groups, and individual counseling, even though I never advertised. My life was moving so fast that I just had to hang on and follow where this energy was leading me. My longing for a spiritual life compelled me to spend every penny on meditation retreats so that I could bathe in the bliss of the inner Self. I was finding it hard to live in the world in the old way, and yet the "new" way still hadn't formed.

This journey took many, many years. After the first year of bliss and light, worldly woes, including financial, relationship, and health difficulties, began to drag me down. I wondered if I had done something wrong to deserve this apparent "fall from Grace." Longing to find the doorway back to that brilliant light, I pursued gurus and teachers, scriptural study, meditations, selfless service, and many techniques that promised to open pathways to God. I even learned to transmute my baser emotions and sexual drive to a higher frequency. Sometimes engaging in these practices would open the door easily; other times the door would not budge.

At first, I enjoyed the game of knocking and trying to find the right "code" to experience the divine door opening. But I realized how much ego I had yet to let go of before the door would stay open. I tried to become aware of this ego and purify myself, which worked for a while, but eventually I saw that my "trying" was what was keeping the door closed. Growing tired of this door game, I wanted to quit; the door was locked and my heart was growing cold. I came to realize that all of my striving was no longer of value.

A deeper purification of my ego was required. Frustrated and miserable, one day I prayed to God, "Please send me a true teacher who is fully purified so that I can be helped and directed to where I need to go next." A part of me resented having to make an effort to return to the light that was previously so available to me, and so becoming a "seeker" felt false. Nonetheless, I realized that I needed to let go of identifying with my awakening experience if I was to be receptive to the blessings and guidance of a teacher.

Some time later, I was supposed to go out with a few friends to a conference that had been planned for weeks, but I felt sick and unable to go. Instead, I chose what I thought would be a relaxing evening listening to a talk by Joseph Chilton Pierce, who was introducing the Siddha Yoga master, Gurumayi Chidvilasananda, to Vancouver. The instant I saw her image on the video screen, I gasped, "Oh my God, that's me!" I knew that I needed to meet her – this was my teacher. After meeting Gurumayi, I felt a sense of renewal and a reminder of *who I really am*. Some of the energies stirring through my body began to balance out.

From that moment on, I spent years studying, traveling, and living in ashrams with her, and I had many powerful and transforming experiences. From Gurumayi's example, I learned how important it was to honour one another and all of life. This was why purification of the ego was so necessary. Even though I knew my true Self, my knowing was obscured by ego tendencies such as unworthiness, doubt, guilt, and pride. For my personality self and God Self to merge as one, cleansing myself of these "ego covers" was required. I was beginning to understand at a deeper level that the true purpose of life really was Love.

I also realized that having an enlightenment experience, awakening, or direct experience of truth, is no ordinary event. Opening to our true Self can come at any time, whether through meditation, childbirth, tragedy, the grace of a true master or any number of other situations, but it requires honouring and nurturing. Once we have experienced the truth, we cannot go back and live the lie. We have a responsibility to the people around us and to the world we live in, which requires seeing ourselves as ambassadors of God's Love. Therefore we must live virtuous lives that encompass selfless service, honesty, seeing the God within everyone, and transmuting every situation to peace and love rather than war and hatred.

We must honour the one Light that is shared by all hearts and that ends with no door of any shape or size, just total stillness, presence, and freedom from the illusion that there is a need for any journey to be taken.

Part

2

The Door Openers

The Being of Light from the far away galaxy asked God another question, "What do these earthlings have to do to open a door to your Light and Love?"

God replied, "There are many doorways through which they can reach me and taste this nectar of Divine Love. All of their sensations, emotions, and feelings can be turned inside themselves. Then, with their "inner eye," they can perceive the Love and Light that awaits them. This Love remains undisturbed by all outer circumstances. But they must learn not to be tricked by what they see with their human eyes. I live in their every breath, every feeling, and every thought. My only desire is to love them with all that I Am."

Opening The Divine Doorway

In the ancient scripture known as the *Spanda Karikas* (Divine Pulsation), it is said that, "All energy is, in its ultimate analysis, only an offshoot of Spiritual energy." [3]

All of life is vibrating with the energy of consciousness. Because we've been taught to live in our minds, we only touch the surface of life. We only believe what we hear, feel, or taste. Thus, we see objects and people at a flat, mundane frequency, which leaves us with a fearful, grasping, painful, and limited perspective. But when we set aside our judgment of what we are feeling or experiencing, and let ourselves rest in the moment, we can dive through the surface into the essence of *who we really are*.

We enter the magic doorway when we allow life to touch us deeply. While I was on one of my meditation retreats, my boyfriend started seeing another woman. Even worse, he asked my best friend to help him support his new woman friend's latest project. I felt so hurt and so betrayed, it was as though I had been stabbed in the heart. I tried to push away the pain so that I could return to a more normal state. When that didn't work, I contracted my body in an effort to numb it, which only made me ill. I realized that I had to find the courage to face the pain. I took a long walk, which is my way of gaining clarity and experiencing my feelings more deeply. I came to a bench and sat down, and began to breathe into all of my hurt, allowing myself to feel it completely. I asked God to help me know the truth of *who I really am* and to show me the teaching embodied in this situation. A little while later, a response came. My heart, belly, and back opened up and the tears spilled forth like a river and so did my love for God. In that sacred moment, I saw that my pain and disappointment were intended to open the door once again to my Divine Self. Then I was able to see my former boyfriend in a new, more compassionate light. I realized that he did not intend to hurt me with his choices; he was just doing what he had to do in his life. Realizing this, I sat on the bench for a long time, holding him in my heart in forgiveness and love.

Every life experience, large and small, can take us to our innermost Self. The comforting chug of a train in the night, the roar of an airplane in the sky, the smell of a beautiful flower, the innocence of a child – these and other apparently ordinary things can inspire the sense of peace that calms our mind and fills our being. When we eat a piece of chocolate or experience an orgasm, we can enjoy the ecstasy of Being. Unfortunately, addiction to these and other substances, habits, or people can arise when we fail to realize that gifts such as sex or chocolate can be doorways to the Divine, but not the Divine itself. The Divine doorway can also fling open when we experience something shocking or challenging such as death or divorce. Having no context for this experience, our mind just stops. Even deep grief can have an unexpected sweetness, if fully embraced.

We are never alone. We are continually swimming in an ocean of consciousness that feeds us as a mother feeds an infant, but if we close ourselves off we will feel starved and dried up. Our refusal to accept Divine nourishment is the root of much of our sorrow. We must catch the current of consciousness that is constantly pulsating beneath all things. We must train ourselves to reach past the surface illusion to the core of all life. Anything that can stop the endless chatter of the mind can open us to God's presence; but we must relax, accept what is, ask for guidance, and then listen to the music of our soul that is continually calling us home. Then we can attune ourselves to the Divine pulsation underlying our outer life experiences.

And so we pass through the magic doorway with open eyes that observe and rest in each moment of life and in each circumstance. In so doing, we draw sustenance from the inner Self, not from the outer form, which either passes away or leaves us barren and empty in the end.

✤Meditation Keys✤

⚬━━🔑 Put a delicious piece of food in your mouth.

⚬━━🔑 Witness all of your physical sensations. Stay with the experience.

⚬━━🔑 Fall deep into the ecstasy.

⚬━━🔑 Now swallow the food and keep the ecstasy that arose from within.

⚬━━🔑 Rest in that deep state of peace, which cannot be taken away or affected by outer circumstances, people or substances.

Embracing the Eternal

Freedom I asked for,
Thinking I could soar
Blissfully above the clamor
And never look back.
Little did I know that freedom means
To dive into the painful darkness itself;
To know it and embrace it all
As the eternal.

From Duality
To Divinity

One of the reasons I was inspired to write this book was to share what I have learned about the power of transmutation[4]. Experiencing enlightenment at the peak of the greatest rage I had ever expressed challenged all of my concepts about right and wrong, good and bad. I saw that anything can be grist for the sacred mill if it accompanies a sincere intention to know the Truth.

In the past, I had always judged myself for "unacceptable" feelings such as anger, fear, jealousy, sadness and so on. Even though I could observe such states and not indulge them, I still felt that they shouldn't be there. I have since learned that anything can take us to our Divine Self when it is allowed to "be." As I have said in the Introduction and will repeat many times throughout this book, the magic key that opens the door to our divinity is a blend of our sincere intention to experience the truth, and our unconditional love and acceptance of whatever arises.

Throughout my life, I have longed to pierce the veils that have kept me from my God Self. But my overactive mind would pull me in the opposite direction, and I would try to satisfy my longing for the Divine with the distractions of the outer world, rather than the urgings of my inner self. This habit created a separation and a tremendous inner tension. Sometimes the tension would build and take the form of dissatisfaction, anger, hatred, fear, abandonment, loneliness, loss, and jealousy. I would try to observe these states passing through, and sometimes that would dissolve them. But there were times when the thoughts created emotions that were too strong to ignore and I felt powerless to combat or transcend them. At such times, I came to understand that I was not in control, and that something larger than me was at the helm. Using my intention to know the Truth, I learned to ride the intensity of the emotion. When the tempestuous emotional seas calmed down, I could divine the purpose of such storms – to wash away my more deeply embedded attachments to things that no longer served me.

For example, there are times when the pressure builds between two people in a relationship. Things reach a point where no matter how faithfully each person observes the negative thoughts or feelings towards the other, or how many yogic techniques each of them uses to control the mind, the negativity won't diminish. Then one day, the energy builds to such a crescendo that everything gets aired out and both people have been cleansed of the limitations that had kept their relationship stuck at a lower level. Thus the stormy emotional wave carries them to a new level of honesty. Just as a rainstorm removes the impurities in the air, so too can inner storms remove the impurities that keep us down and separate from God.

On one occasion, while living in a beautiful ashram with my meditation Master, Gurumayi Chidvilasananda, with whom I studied for 16 years, the inner tensions built to such an extent that I was pushed through the divine door. On the surface, everything seemed peaceful, but the spiritual practices of selfless service, meditation, and chanting, and the grace of the Guru put great strain on everyone's ego, including mine. At times, we all seemed a little mad. The crushing pressure on the contracted mind was meant only to relieve us of the veils that kept us believing we were limited beings rather than divine beings. Nonetheless, the pressure, designed to work on each person according to his or her particular need for growth, felt awful. I loved meditation but I had great aversion for the noise and busyness at the ashram. My aversion reached a peak one day when I was riding on a hot, crowded, poorly ventilated bus, feeling overcome by body odour, incessant chatter, and continual bumping up against my fellow passengers. For my highly sensitive nervous system, it all felt like torture; every moment felt like an eternity. A mantra was playing constantly and repetitively. I felt that if I heard one more "Om," I would tear the speaker from the wall. I prayed fervently to God, "Please help me. I can't bear this anymore." The internal and external pressure built to such an intensity that just as I was about to lose it, in what seemed like a split second, my mind imploded into a whole other state of awareness. Rather than being bumped around, I was being carried on a gentle wave. All my irritation dissolved into peace and love. The mantras became a heavenly chorus and I felt at one with everyone on the bus. It was as if the pressure placed on the coal of my mind created a diamond of consciousness.

I was no longer just a body. I became pure awareness.

Later, while taking a walk, another veil dropped. All the leaves on the trees shone with incredible brilliance. The sky, the pebbles, and the road became one with the shimmering Love. I felt as if I was touching the entire world with my hand, which was really a heart. I saw the face of God in all creation. I knew in that moment that I and everything and everybody in this universe are in God's heart, as undulating consciousness. I felt deep gratitude and love, and I saw all of my unwanted pain as the pain of birth and the pain of death, and that entering into these tunnels with open and witnessing eyes, brought me to the light. Having witnessed the face of God in everything, my ideas about what was "spiritual" and what was "worldly" slowly began to dissolve. Labels no longer held any power over me. The concepts or boxes in which I had previously felt comfortable, were gone. The old me began to feel like a cardboard cutout animated by the creative power. Every moment and every place was of God's essence. I saw how I was truly a part of the whole and not separate from anything; I was not different from others.

I saw the one soul permeating throughout All That Exists. I saw that God has no judgment over us, and that all that we experience can be used as fertilizer to yield bountiful crops. I saw the only thing in us that needs changing is the belief that we are separate from God. The only purpose of our experiences is to push sufficiently hard on our self-judgment and perceived limitations, that any beliefs that separate us from God and each other can be shattered.

✤Meditation Keys✤

Recall a time when you felt strong irritation.

Where were you at the time? Who and/or what surrounded you? Relive this moment.

Remove the label "irritation" from this feeling and just explore the sensations that you are having.

Rest deeply in the sensations that you are experiencing.

Ask to know the truth of who you really are.

Be open to receiving the answer whether it comes to you as a physical feeling, a sense of love and light, peace, joy, stillness, or a deep knowing.

Receive this gift knowing that God is in everything.

When Magic Died

When I was small, everything was magic
New, wondrous, fresh, exciting, free.
Then they told me:
Don't feel this way.
Don't think that way.
This is good. That is bad.
You are right. You are wrong.
Confused I became -
And then my wondrous world became tainted
With labels and judgments that I didn't understand.

Slowly the magic disappeared
And the labels and boxes neatly defined my reality.
Sadder and older, I plod through life
And my label shakes hands with all the other labels,
And so we agree to pretend
That the magic is a fantasy
And that freedom is only for the mad.

Removing The Labels

Labeling ourselves and our world, and then believing these labels to be real, is the greatest obstruction to the open door of consciousness. We perceive something, and instead of observing it as a stream of consciousness, we label it, identify with it, resist it, and then crystallize the moment, person, or event.

I once met a Chinese teacher at a time when I needed to gain a deeper understanding of ego. My intuition told me that I was to meet someone to learn something, but I had no idea who that was or how this meeting would come about. I prayed and asked for help, and the very next day, a client handed me a check for $1000 and said, "Take a trip." I accepted the gift with gratitude but had no idea where to go. The following day, "Arizona" flashed through my mind and so I booked and boarded a flight to Scottsdale. There I rented an apartment and waited. After a few days, I accepted an invitation from an acquaintance, who asked me to accompany her to meet with a Chinese Chi Gong master. Walking into the room, I saw a powerful Chinese woman who reminded me of a fire goddess. She looked at me intently and a surge of power passed between us. I will always remember her core teaching: "The ego grabs the garbage."

In the short time that I was with her, I reached a new understanding that our thoughts about who we are or what our present circumstances mean, or what is right or what is wrong, pass by constantly, not unlike clouds or radio waves. If we have a negative thought, it is not a problem. It's what we do with such thought forms that gives rise to painful emotions or a limited negative reality. When we grab hold of a passing thought and say, "Yes, this is me, I am bad, I am unworthy," then our consciousness reflects that belief and we experience a reality of unworthiness.

To become free of labels is to become a Master, witnessing the movement of consciousness as the clouds go by, knowing that blue sky exists eternally in the background. We need to identify ourselves with the blue sky, not the clouds that constantly dissipate and change. When we don't witness our thoughts and judgments, we become the labels and live in our egos. The problems begin when we believe that every thought, feeling, and sensation that appears belongs to us – when we tell ourselves that this is my feeling, my thought, my body, my image... These emotions, feelings, thoughts, and bodies no more belong to us than a cloud belongs to the sky. Imagine the blue sky perceiving a passing cloud, and then contracting itself and saying, "I am not this expansiveness; I am that cloud!" Absurd though it is, we do it continually. "I am not Love and pure consciousness, I am a woman," or "I am a wealthy entrepreneur," or "I am a sad person," or "I am a good and happy person," or "I am an alcoholic," or "I am an intellectual"... We are so identified with our labels, that we often deny and misunderstand ego, assuming it to mean self-aggrandizement. We think that to view ourselves to be Love and pure consciousness means that we are conceited. However, ego is anything that makes us believe that we are just a cloud separate from that clear blue sky of consciousness; this includes beliefs about our unworthiness as well as beliefs about being more special than others. As we remove the labels by not grabbing hold of them as they stream through our thoughts, we may still experience old, toxic labels we've previously grabbed. These labels may have become fixed and are now being mirrored by people in everyday situations. Recognizing that the appearance of these reflections, feelings, thoughts, and/or physical sensations reflects a cleansing of our energy field can help us release them. Discharging these old, heavy identities is like allowing poison to leave our system, freeing us to feel light and joyful like the infinite blue sky that we know ourselves to be.

�֍Meditation Keys – Removing the Labels�֍

🔑 *Think of one negative thought about yourself that you have believed to be true.*

🔑 *Spend a few moments contemplating this negative thought form that you have chosen.*

🔑 *Let yourself fully experience the belief that you really are that thought form. Notice the emotional state that it produces within you.*

🔑 *Now return again to who you were before the label or thought form arose. Witness the sequence of events that takes place:*

> *The thought passes through.*
> *The ego grabs the thought and identifies with it.*
> *You now believe you are bad, ugly, unloving or stupid or whatever the negative label or thought form may be.*
> *Emotion wells up and you feel terrible.*
> *You feel worthless and abandoned by God.*

🔑 *Now start over again.*

🔑 *The thought passes through.*

🔑 *Witness it passing through you like a cloud and let it pass.*

🔑 *Don't grab it.*

🔑 *Recognize that this is where true freedom lies!*

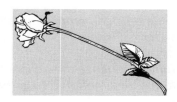

One Kiss

One kiss blows life into nothingness
One kiss and what was dead comes alive
One kiss and the velvety petals of a ruby red rose
Emerge from the darkness
And reach yearningly for the light.
One kiss and a breathing, living, sumptuous child
Arises from flesh
One kiss and the skies open and drop joyous tears
Onto the painter's creation
One kiss and that which lived must die
One kiss and that which died is reborn anew
And vibrates in the ocean of forever.
One kiss and all that appeared to be
Returns to just one kiss.

The Kiss

Just before I began writing this book, I came down with the flu. Breathing was a struggle, and the pain in my body was unbearable. I was so ill for so long that I didn't think I would ever recover. I let go of all hope of surviving – I had no choice.

I soon came to realize that my lack of hope was actually a blessing. Having given up, I could accept what was being presented in that moment – the possibility that I was very sick and might die. With that acceptance, my body relaxed and, for the first time in a long time, I was able to pray. With all of my heart and soul, I asked for understanding as to the purpose of this illness. After a while, I felt warm all over, and I experienced something kissing me. Every aching muscle was being kissed and loved and soothed. I felt so full, so loved, and so blessed. I had received an answer to my prayer and my feeling of having been abandoned in my illness dissolved. I saw that I really am in a relationship with God, as we all are. Our relationship with God is no different from any other in the sense that we must learn to communicate our heartfelt needs, as we would to anyone whom we love and who loves us. The sense of being kissed has never left me and it has become one of the barometers to indicate my receptivity to God's love. After "the kiss," I began to heal very quickly. As I was recovering, this book was conceived.

How can we bring the kiss of God into our daily lives? How can we love ourselves as God loves us? My illness taught me that surrendering to what is, along with seeking a higher understanding, can take us to God. We must truly desire to discover the higher reason for every situation that we are in. If our desires and goals are strictly material, then we might find it harder to access a more refined state of consciousness. If we see the world as objects and circumstances that we must acquire, change or manipulate, or if we think our true reason for being is to attain some worldly desire or goal, we will miss the small, quiet voice inside of us that always seeks to expand our perspective.

Entering the magic doorway means living every moment in relationship with God or our higher Self, recognizing that every little event or circumstance reflects the quality of that relationship. How do we treat each person we meet? Do we uplift them with our love, or judge them as inept or a bother? How do we respect our living space? Do we see it as a temple for God or a place to crash or showoff? How do we work with others? Is our ego in control or our love? How do we treat our own mind and feelings? Do we treat them with respect as we would a friend? Do we listen with an open heart, or do we get angry with ourselves for having bothersome feelings and thoughts? Do we wish they would go away, and then distract ourselves so as not to feel them? How do we nourish ourselves? Is it with good, balanced food, or is it with food that creates chaos in mind and body? These are only a few examples of how we can contemplate our lives, moment by moment. In so doing, we open the magic door to the wisdom of the inner Self, and see everything we encounter as another reflection of God.

Unconditional acceptance of what is, and the intention to know the truth, is the key. Feeling victimized by life is forgetting that we truly have all the power we need within our hearts. Every moment at its essence is another opportunity to enter the vast love of God. Memorable events such as marriage or childbirth are obvious avenues, but so are "ordinary" experiences such as a visit with a beloved friend, a flower, a beautiful scent, a rainbow, a pebble, a warm blanket, nourishing food… Even events we might judge as tragic, such as divorce, the death of a child, a terminal illness, and other kinds of losses can take us to God. Whether we experience wealth or poverty, joy or sorrow, warmth or cold, chaos or quietude, our judgments must be set aside and the moment itself must be embraced with an open heart. With our love shining, all distinctions, positive and negative, disappear, and all that remains is the constant, unchanging kiss of God.

✤Meditation Keys – The Kiss✤

⚷ *Day One. See every object, person and situation in life as your own God Self, abundantly presenting you with the opportunity to enter the magic door.*

⚷ *Day Two. Spend an entire day respecting everyone – friend, stranger, or "enemy." Respect every object you encounter – your car, your house, your computer, a pencil, a stone… See how that feels.*

⚷ *Day Three. Become like a child again, exploring this world with eyes of wonder, as if everything in it were brand new.*

The Gift of Love

*I lie on the warm, green grass
And I watch a beautiful flower offer and open itself to a
golden bee
As the clouds offer their drops of nourishment to the
earth.
Then I turn onto my side and behold a swarm of ants
Carrying little grains of sand to build their hill.
I turn to my other side,
And wrapped in great tenderness,
A child feeds at its mother's breast.
Then I look at my own hand
And discover how beautifully it was designed
For this Love that knows nothing but giving.*

Love & Service

ne day, sitting in the park, I contemplated the question, "What is life?" Then I looked around and saw bees extracting nectar from flowers. I saw the sun shining and giving sustenance to the Earth. I saw how everything in nature gives and receives in an infinite number of ways. Glancing down at my aerobic shoe, I saw how all the weaving in the front was designed for comfort and protection, and that the heel was built up so my ankles would be supported. Somebody had designed those shoes to ensure another's comfort and safety.

In that moment, my question was answered. Life is service, and service is love. Whether we realize it or not, we are serving all the time, in an infinite number of ways – at our jobs, with our children, with our families, with the stranger to whom we give directions… Sadly, we never feel that we are worth anything unless we are doing something that impresses others, or that makes a lot of money, but each of us is here to give love or service in his or her own way. One of us might be here to be a movie star and to stir others' hearts. Another might be here to be a farmer – to till the earth and help nourish people. Yet another might be a teacher, a doctor, a garbage collector or a bus driver. However, the belief that our worthiness comes solely from what we do, is a big trap. If our life is on a down swing, and our productivity and finances are not what they were in the past, our self-esteem can plummet. I know this from experience. My writing, counseling, and group facilitation work do not provide a predictable income and, as a result, I have sometimes felt that what I have to offer has no value. At such times, I am like many others who forget that their very being has an impact on other people; true service may be something so simple and natural that its value is overlooked.

Part of why we feel so lost and in pain is that we have forgotten *who we really are*. This is comparable to a bee forgetting its job and wandering aimlessly around while all the flowers are waiting to be pollinated. Or the clouds holding on to the rain when the earth is crying for water. Forgetting to nourish each other, we humans can do things because we have to or for"what's in it for us." In so doing, we forget the original Self.

The Christmas movie, *It's a Wonderful Life,* is a perfect illustration of what it means to serve. George, the main character, is so convinced that his life has been useless and that he is worth more dead than alive that he considers taking his own life. As he is about to jump off the bridge, he fervently prays to God for help. An angel appears and shows George how the people in his life would have fared without him. George is in disbelief at how many people he has unknowingly helped, people who would otherwise have had terrible lives. He sees how his seemingly insignificant acts of kindness and understanding had a profound impact on many others. He re-enters his life with great joy, renewal, gratitude and love, knowing for certain that he isn't the failure he had once thought he was, but that his life is truly of great service and value.

We are already perfect, whoever we are, in whatever form – weak or strong, intelligent or "slow," happy or sad. No matter how we look or how we feel, whether we have been mistreated or indulged, our only purpose is to serve.

If we have children, we must see mothering or fathering as holy service, instead of feeling inadequate because of being *just* a parent. If our job isn't glamorous, and we feel it is beneath us, we must start serving and treating everyone and everything at work with respect, and see how different we feel. If we are in emotional pain, we must see it as the pain of all humanity. Then we can receive the next person who comes our way with compassion, recognizing how our pain links us to one another and to God. If we are sick, we must learn who we are while ill, and accept the pain to establish a communion with our soul. If we are out of work and feeling useless and unworthy, then we must make ourselves useful. Easing a neighbour's day with a kind word or a listening ear, moving a banana peel so that someone doesn't slip, helping an elder to cross the street... As we open to our current experience and its opportunities for service, we connect to the hearts of all others.

We are needed every day in one way or another, no matter who we are, or what we are, or in what stage of life
we find ourselves. There is no service unworthy of God,
and everything we do with love, whether it is a little or
a lot, is true service. And that is the most infallible way
into the divine Self.

✤Meditation Keys – Love and Service✤

☜ Reflect on the activities of your day. Has this day
presented any opportunities for service?

☜ Make a list of ways that you have served others as well as
times in which you have ignored the call to service.

☜ Try to improve the next day.

☜ Every day for a week, list the ways that you have served and
the times that you have ignored the call to service.

☜ At the end of the week, notice the progress that you have
made.

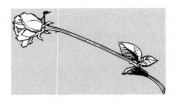

An Ecstatic Feast

Oh, to be a human!
To touch, smell, taste, feel;
To run naked in the open, pungent air,
To be showered upon by the warm rain,
To see miraculous beauty with these sacred eyes,
To be caressed by warm breezes,
To inhale velvety flowers painted by heaven,
To taste a sweet, juicy fruit
That magically appears on a branch
As an offering from God;
To breathe the unseen as it invites us to ride on its
back
Into worlds yet unknown,
And to dance and spin, recklessly and freely,
Drinking from the vehicle of flesh and bones
Into a frenzied state of divine ecstasy.

The Doorway of the Senses

od has given us so much. We can taste delicious food, drink clear water, make love and experience ecstasy, touch a baby's soft skin... We can smell sweet jasmine, fresh-baked bread, or new-mown hay; we can hear stirring music, crashing waves, or birdsong; we can see sunsets, beautiful art, or fields of daisies... Within our own bodies, we are truly living in the Garden of Eden.

Unfortunately, we tend to take our senses for granted, and look outside ourselves for fulfillment. Overlooking the amazing miracle that we are, we treat ourselves like machines rather than works of art. We would prefer to travel to Mars and Venus than open the doorway to our own divinity. We avoid the glory of our senses by thinking about the future or living in the past, and not being present to the moment that we live in now. This creates a numbness, which blocks our joy. A simple cup of coffee can become pure nectar when we arrive at the place beyond thought. One day I was washing some broccoli, allowing myself to slow down so that all I could feel was the broccoli in my hands and the sensation of the water washing over it. I was so focused on this task that I became the broccoli. Great love welled up inside of me and I lost all sense of separation between this vegetable and myself. I felt something like an orgasm running through every part of my body. Since that time, I've always enjoyed broccoli! If we simply slow down to savour all the beauty that is inside of us, and in those we love, we wouldn't need sex therapists either! We already are what we seek.

When we begin to realize *who we really are*, our cup is always filled; it has never been empty. The joy we seek from the outside never stays with us for long, but the joy we can access from our own being is eternal. Even if we are unwell or paralyzed and unable to fully appreciate this glory of the senses, there is a level of sensation that we can feel throughout our lives. It transcends pain and sorrow. It is the sensation of our true Self.

All these sensations originate from the very source of life, so it only makes sense that to keep the senses clear and sharp, we must return each day to the Source to replenish these gifts and remind ourselves of who we really are. The senses are the outward dance of the eternal. We have been given the opportunity to separate from the Source by becoming a body, and through that very body we can use our senses to pay homage to our divine Self. The form has been created so it can take great pleasure in worshiping the formless.

The Saints say that there are souls lining up for the experience of a human birth, so they can feel what we feel. We must respect our gifts by never forgetting why we took a human birth. When we remember that this sensation-blessed human body is here to worship its own God Self, every breath we take is a miracle.

✤Meditation Keys – The Doorway of the Senses✤

Take a few moments and think of someone you love – a partner, parent, child, friend, pet...

Envision this being in front of you. Feel the sensations of love that arise.

Keep focused on the love as it moves through you.

Remove the image or outer focus of this loved one and stay with your inner experience.

Recognize that the sensation of love that we attribute to the outer form is in fact the love of God coming through that very form.

Let this remind you that the senses are the outward dance of the eternal.

Love will always find you

There is nothing you can do to escape love.
You can run from it, deny it,
Scream at it, or stomp on it -
It will not go away.
It will chase you relentlessly,
Torture you, tease you.
Its forms will change.
It will look like fear, hatred,
Sadness, pain or joy.
It will look like friend or foe.
It will look like sun or moon.
It will burn you. It will cool you.
It will twist you around
You cannot run away.
It permeates your every cell.
It breathes you.
It makes you walk, see,
Feel and think.
It makes you live. It makes you die.
It is your very Self, so why run away?
There is no escape
From this prison of ecstasy.

From Emotion To Devotion

Emotions are the beacons of the soul's longing for God. Their purpose is to take us to the Truth of *who we really are*. In the enlightenment intensive at which I was contemplating the question, "Who am I?" my emotions became so strong that I thought I would blow up. But at the point of my greatest rage, I did explode – not into destructiveness but into an awakened state. That day I learned something important about the power of emotion combined with an intention to know the truth. I wanted to experience *who I really am* so acutely that I became enraged. My clear intention created a conduit for my emotions to rise to a higher frequency, so that anger was transmuted into enlightenment.

Later on, I was relieved to come across this particular

scripture that provided context for my uncommonly intense experience. In *Spanda Karikas*, Jaideva Singh writes:

> "In intense emotional experience, whether of anger, joy, fear or acute mental impasse, all the extroverted mental activities come to a dead stop... It is only when this whirligig stops, when the mind is stilled that we are in a fit condition to have an experience of Reality or the Spanda principle, if we are properly oriented towards it... intense emotional experiences, of themselves, bring the squirrel-like activities of the mind to a dead halt. That is the psychological moment for catching the vibration of the inner Reality...if one is properly introverted to be blessed with its vision. This opportunity is not open to all; it is only to those who are eagerly waiting for its reception. [5] "

Emotion without direction or awareness can be destructive, hurtful, and exhausting. But these same emotions, when accompanied by a focused desire to know the Truth, can propel us through the doorway to our divine self. Just as our sensations are a portal into our deepest self, so too are emotions, as they have a very dynamic nature.

Many spiritual paths suggest that emotions be pushed away or denied as they are seen as a distraction. In certain cases, this is true; however, emotions are difficult for most people to move beyond. But if we take hold of our intention to know the Truth and embrace emerging emotions as part of God, then they will take us to Love's door more readily than any mind-induced repression. Emotion truly is a doorway to devotion.

We do not need to go looking for emotions to transmute. If they arise in our daily life or meditations, and refuse to pass by, then they need to be moved to a higher frequency of Love. To do this, we must remember that emotions are beacons of the souls' longing for God. Nothing is wasted if our intention is to know our deepest *Self*; any intense feeling can open the door to truth.

I have experienced great sadness in my life; I have sometimes felt as though I could not live another day. At such times, I have even questioned my meditation practice and my commitment to God. My grief has arisen from my constant, sometimes painful longing to merge with God. Compounding my grief are worldly privations – money issues, health difficulties, and the loss of friends through change, sickness or death.

Sometimes we find ourselves immersed in emotions that feel unrelenting. Suicidal thoughts are not uncommon as we watch old identities crumble. Because of my all-pervading sense of the impermanence of life, loss of identity has been a common experience. Then, just at the point of collapsing with grief, I have experienced a deep upsurge of divine Love wrapping its arms around me. In that moment I know that the pain has not been negative, but another doorway into my divine Self.

Every emotion we experience can be transmuted into Love, since Love is the only reality. In our struggle to connect with the Love that underlies daily life, we play hide and seek, trying to find the hidden opening which

will return us to Love. Refraining from judging or label-
ing is the most important way to experience this Love.

Every emotion is the Self trying to speak to us; it is not
something to be analyzed or figured out. We've been
taught to deny or act out our emotions. Pleasant ones
are acceptable; angry or fearful ones are unacceptable.
Yet, if we can take the emotional body to a higher frequency by remembering that all emotions are beacons
of the soul's longing for God, we can become
alchemists, and through our anger, fear, joy or grief, we
can touch the essence of Being. Having a full range of
emotions and feelings brings more power into the body.
By directing everything to the Source instead of blaming ourselves or someone else, we become free to
dance the dance for which we have incarnated.

I have always been an intense personality; I feel everything deeply. When I love someone, I love him or her to
my core. When I suffer, it is excruciating. More than I
would care to admit, emotions have ruled my life. I have
hated myself for feeling so much, harshly comparing
myself with others who seemed to feel little or nothing
at all. I also have a psychic "gift" that allows me to dis-
cern others' thoughts and feel their emotions. This has
been beneficial in my work as a counselor, but in everyday life, I have needed to withdraw from those people
who might not understand the suffering involved in
feeling so deeply. Over time, I have begun to realize that
my emotions, which have seemed like a curse, have
often guided me to find my heart and to help others
find theirs. Needing an anchor in the storm of my feelings, I have used the pain as a teacher and have learned
a lot about human and divine Love.

Just as one day it rains and the next day it is sunny, emotions do not stay forever. The true Self exists in a state of balance or equanimity – unchanging, always present, and unaffected by the waves of the world. Because we are living in a body, we get to play with the whole range of human experience, which can be highly charged at times. If we can be unafraid of our emotions, we can have so much more compassion for others in their pain, fear, or sadness. The more I embrace my own emotions, without judgment, the more I am able to see the divinity in everyone around me, regardless of their costume or what they might be acting out. But most of all, I have learned that when a strong feeling or aversion to something or someone arises, I have an opportunity to face myself deeply and walk through the Divine Door and into my heart.

✤Meditation Keys – From Emotion to Devotion✤

⊙━▅ *Spend a day simply watching your negative emotions as they arise.*

⊙━▅ *Instead of judging yourself for having them, lovingly embrace these emotions as opportunities to practice compassion for yourself.*

Anger

Anger can be a difficult emotion to transmute; it is often judged in our culture, and it is frequently abused. At the root of much of our anger are our unmet desires. We get angry when someone fails to behave in the way that we want, or when something we want fails to materialize. In other words, we are likely to get angry when our expectations and desires are unmet. Anger can also be a reaction to deeper feelings that are too frightening to acknowledge.

Anger also comes with a great purpose. It is our sword of discernment, to establish our boundaries so that we may know what fits for us and what does not. When we begin to open to our true Self, and our anger has been unexpressed for a long time, we may feel enraged when repressed memories surface. After many years of suppression, self-judgment, guilt, not speaking the truth, and believing in false concepts, low-grade anger can erupt into higher-grade anger, as it purges our suppressed feelings. Rage can serve to clear away old conditioning that does not serve us. If we have spent a lifetime lying to ourselves and suppressing our feelings, anger will have a lot of work to do and the process will often be uncomfortable. It is important to be aware of what is happening, so as not to feel victimized or to victimize others in this process.

Inherent in anger is power. Such power can be used like a knife – to heal or to kill. When we remove the label from anger, we are left with a raw power that can be directed toward the light. The day before I give a workshop, I often feel tremendous anger. When I remove the label, I realize the energy is building in me to create a strong channel for Truth. I no longer see this energy as anger, but as power. When we welcome our anger rather than trying to eliminate it, it becomes our ally, rather than an enemy that we have to suppress or act out unconsciously.

�֍Meditation Keys – Anger�֍

🔑 Recall an incident in which a desire was thwarted and you became angry.

🔑 If the desire had been met, what did you expect to experience?

🔑 If there is another way to have that experience, identify what that would be.

🔑 Then act on it.

🔑 If the feeling of anger persists in your body, remove the label, "anger," and feel the power that is moving through you.

🔑 As though wielding a sword, redirect your intention from having a desire met to asking to know the higher truth of this situation.

🔑 Ask that this process be guided by the hand of God, or by the higher Self, so as to realize the highest outcome.

Fear

Once I was in a small airplane with a friend who was terrified of flying. If anyone spoke to her during the flight, she would become so angry that she would yell and hurl obscenities. This was completely out of character, but she was so afraid that the only way that she could express it was through her anger. I have always remembered this as a great example of how fear is often beneath anger.

Our entire world is fear-based, yet we deny this in order to get through the day. But we have locks on our doors or even alarm systems to protect us. We have banks for our money. We run around, desperately trying to make ends meet, or if we have our basic necessities, we're afraid of losing them. We fear for the safety of our children, our families, and our mates. We have fears about our work and our health. Now we are afraid to travel because of terrorism. Many of us fear natural disasters. Fear of being alone, fear getting old. Many are afraid of life itself, and most everyone is afraid of death. The list could go on forever.

Most of us live in fear because we think we have to do everything ourselves. But because everyone around us is also afraid, nobody is available to remind us that we are a part of God and that love, grace, and trust await us when we look within.

Survival fear is our biggest fear, since we are still living in an animal body, responding to animal desires and needs. We are evolving at this time from an animal

consciousness to a human consciousness, from material, form-oriented consciousness to a divine consciousness, but until we are continually connected to the
heart of God, we will always have fear.

Healthy fear directs us from potentially harmful situations or people; but the fear referred to here is the fear
of life and of death. Take away our denial of death and
all that is left is fear; we think we are only the body and
therefore fear everything that is potentially harmful.
The fear of walking alone without God in our hearts is
the most terrifying fear of all. Our control, beliefs, and
habitual ways of being must transform in order to make
the transition from "my will" to "Thy Will." The transmutation of the ego is the end of fear.

We often run away from fear, denying its existence and
then acting out other behaviors, which help us to avoid
feeling it. These include overindulging in food, alcohol,
drugs, sex, work, or escaping into other peoples' lives
through television or movies. There is an infinite number of such neurotic behaviors that we see all the time
in ourselves and in one other; all of them originate from
fear. We will never be free until we look fear in the face
and have the courage to feel and witness it. Otherwise,
we are the performer who feels stage fright, but rather
than feeling the fear and performing anyway, he or she
runs away from the stage. Running from fear is running
from life. Running from fear is running from God.

Moving toward the flame of God is one of the most
frightening things to do because it means ending a way
of life that was neither real nor true, and facing ourselves in very vulnerable ways. The light of God is very

bright and traveling towards it takes great courage. But when we take this step, we realize that fear is a paper dragon; it is only the energy of God in a contracted form. Fear inhabits the past or the future. When we live in the present moment, fear dissolves and the door opens to Love.

✦Meditation Keys - Fear✦

⚷ *Spend a few moments and connect to something in your life that gives rise to fear.*

⚷ *Notice your fear. See how fear eats at you, chases you, will not let you be. Take your time here.*

⚷ *Look the fear in the face and feel its energy run through you.*

⚷ *Remove the label "fear" and just see and experience this pure energy running through your body.*

⚷ *See this energy as the energy of God coursing through your body, awakening and enlivening sleeping cells.*

⚷ *Remember that whenever you experience fear, that it is really God coming to you as an opportunity to expand from your contracted state.*

ſadneſſ & Grief

Sadness and grief can take us to God and the Self. As we release our identification with our personality, we are often left with sadness, as we would be with any loss. Following my awakening experience, my personality self suffered a lot when my identity changed from someone who received a lot of respect from the world to someone who probably seemed a little mad at times. Stepping to a different drummer from the mainstream, sometimes I would grieve at not being able to "dance" or interact as I once had; what stirred me now was so different from the rhythms of the world that still moved my friends. I would feel sad as I watched my old life and its joys disappear. I would have thoughts like, "How did I end up here after all the promise of my previous life?"

But the transition from a life engrossed in the world to a life focused on the spirit takes time; the sadness comes from looking at the past rather then at the many gifts offered in the moment. Where my identification once sat, emptiness remained, leaving me free to be filled with God's love.

Sometimes when I'm deeply sad, I offer my pain directly to the Source so that God can fill my heart with Love. Because we are open when our hearts hurt, God can more easily touch us. We are softer, more pliant, as in this passage from *The Prophet* by Kahlil Gibran: "He threshes to make you naked. He kneads you until you are pliant. He sifts you to free you from your husks, so that you can become sacred bread for God's sacred feast." (6)

Grief often arises as the Sculptor chisels us to a new and unknown form. Within our sadness, there is great and deep Love.

✦Meditation Keys – Sadness and Grief✦

O━🔧 *Think of a current situation that brings up sadness for you.*

O━🔧 *Notice where this sadness sits or rests in your being.*

O━🔧 *Breathe into this sadness.*

O━🔧 *Take the label "sadness" away and sink into the feeling that remains.*

O━🔧 *If any tears arise, allow yourself to fully experience and express them.*

O━🔧 *Allow the depth of this energy to embrace you.*

O━🔧 *Keep going until you merge into the deep Love that awaits you in the package of sadness.*

Joy

Joy is the essence of our true Self. When something or someone brings us joy, the joy arises from inside of us, not from the outer form, as is commonly believed. Our true essence is a constant experience of bliss that remains whether we are sad, happy, or fearful. By connecting with our highest Self, we can feel joy in the midst of any emotion or storm; we can move through hard times with grace and self-love.

True joy is a moment of ecstasy that bubbles up from inside us, making us think of God and feel gratitude. Worldly joy, on the other hand, is a temporary feeling that arises because a desire has been met. But if we can capture that worldly joy and turn it back to the Source by remembering that all emotions are beacons of the souls' longing for God, then all of our joy will be seen as God's joy and will remain with us forever.

✤Meditation Keys – Joy✤

Experiencing joy should not be an accidental occurrence.

Think of an activity that allows you to experience the essence of your true Self, whether it's meditation, chanting, prayer, yoga, going for a walk in nature, or a long run – whatever appeals to you.

Vow to do this activity at least once every day.

Remember to see the joy that you derive from this activity as not coming from the activity itself. It is a revelation of the joy that already exists within you.

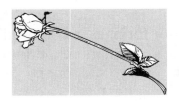

Unravelling the Costume

*Oh such sorrow to be human
To try and fit a mold, a box, an image.
Oh such sorrow
To be caught in the worldly web.*

*Let me throw myself down at Your Feet
So you can erase all those false notions I have.
Make me remember, for I have forgotten
And have fallen victim of this costume I wear.
Make me remember my oneness with You.
Merge me forever into Your Infinite Love.
Dissolve me into You forever.
Never to return again to the great sleep.*

Transcending Outer Appearances

𝕴 once had a dream in which a friend and I were at a party where there was a machine that could alter our appearance. My friend went first and I watched him become a midget. In every other way, he was exactly the same person, but he looked entirely different. I wasn't sure I wanted to play but, unable to resist the fascination of this machine, I found myself under its lights being transformed from a slender, fair-haired woman to a large, dark-haired woman with big lips. It was strange yet somehow normal. My friend and I returned to the party and I recall walking by a mirror and seeing myself with a mane of black hair and thick lips, while feeling the same inside. I was just wearing another costume. When I awakened, I realized the importance of this dream and its message about appearances.

My entire early life was based on being attractive, successful, appropriate, and securing others' approval for all of these things. I constantly measured and compared myself and endeavored to be more attractive, successful, wealthy, and appropriate than anyone else. I was lost in outer appearances. I was not free to be me and to follow my inner impulses. I found myself directed by the media and by the expectations and judgments of others. I believed that if I upheld the external standards I'd set for myself, love would be mine.

Mostly, I felt fear – fear of losing love that was conditional upon upholding an image of success. I felt trapped, yet I defended my actions to myself in order to keep the structure intact. I didn't know that my entire identity was just another costume and had little to do with the real me. After all, it complied with what seemed desirable in our culture.

This emphasis on the external has remained, despite many years of meditation and a number of mystical experiences that have revealed that I am more than just the body. But the ego programming is so strong and so deep, that it is very difficult to free ourselves. This is why we undergo major life transformations that cause us to fall through the illusion of the old life. As we fall, we destroy its structure and foundation, making way for a true life to begin. In my early life, I felt strong and confident in just about anything that I did; I rarely doubted myself, was aware of my many gifts, and would not hesitate to give them expression. I felt special. This afforded me self-reliance, which was great for moving projects forward. The down side was that I felt separate from other people. After many years of spiritual practice, my false confidence began to wane. My ego was being transformed from that of someone who believed that she was special to someone who knows that we are all special in God's eyes, regardless of outer appearances. We tend to believe we are the body/mind alone. We habitually believe that what we see is what we get. This kind of thinking creates a terrifying reality based only on fear and lack. All of life is a preparation for death. Each day the body deteriorates. In a world focused upon high gloss and polished body images, this can be extremely painful. If we believe that outer appearances are the only truth, then there isn't much worth living for. Appearances can disappear very quickly, leaving us clinging, angry, fearful, greedy, cruel, and impatient. Thus we try harder to be better, healthier, smarter, quicker, richer, more brilliant robotic beings, leaving little time for simple truth.

Jesus said, "You must become like little children to enter the Kingdom of Heaven." Children love to play with animals or with their friends; they need very little to be happy. Love allows them to flourish. They find so much magic in the so-called mundane. They scream when they're angry, cry when they're sad, and then, moments later, they laugh. They know when an environment isn't right for them. Unlike children, we deny our feelings and intuitions in favor of the worldly image; then we take anti-depressants to fight the depression of the malnourished psyche. We must return to that childlike sense of what is true for us based on our inner knowing.

We have come into life at this time for a great purpose; we can no longer hide behind our costumes. We must be mindful of the reality of death, which pierces the appearances. If a tidal wave or earthquake were to hit, all so-called powerful appearances would dissolve. Who would we be then? Who are we now? The aliens in the movie, *Cocoon*, had more advanced ways then the earthlings, but looked the same. The big difference was that every evening the aliens would unzip their outward human costume from head to foot, and a ball of light would emerge. Once the outer human forms were gone, all that remained were identical balls of brilliant light. We too can play with our costumes, knowing that they can be rearranged and taken off at will. We can be actors in this play, rather than prisoners. As we shed our outer appearances, we too are left with the oneness that brings us to the light and love that never goes away, no matter what costume we wear.

✦Meditation Keys – Transcending Outer Appearances✦

🔑 *Pretend you are an alien who has just come to Earth on an assignment. You are already free and know who you are. You know that you are nothing but pure light.*

🔑 *Whatever Earth assignment you have been given, whether it be a lawyer, wife, garbage collector or farmer, whether it be male or female, see yourself putting on the costume to play your part joyously.*

🔑 *You are not bound by whatever part you are playing, so you can play like a child, even with others who believe they really are their role.*

🔑 *You are also free to let your strong points of view relax since it's only a game anyway.*

🔑 *Practise putting your costume on in the morning and taking it off at night so you are constantly freeing yourself every day.*

False Promises

What is this mirage?
My heart and soul are so dry.
I need this Divine water but all that I see are pictures,
Images, roles, thoughts.
I reach out anyway to grab them,
Just in case I can squeeze some water out of them.
As I come closer, this mirage looks so delicious,
So wet, so satisfying.
I can feel my thirst
On the verge of being quenched,
As I bring the bitter cup to my lips.
I am burned, parched, dryer than before.
I've been tricked again by the false promises of these
concepts,
And the emptiness of thoughts
And my soul is left bereft without the Divine nectar,
So I continue to seek.
Sad, disappointed, and angry,
Please show me where I can quench my thirst,
Everywhere I look I see only illusion,
Is there not a door to take me from this dream?

Exposing
The Concepts

Depression/anxiety is one of the major diseases of our time. So many of us are like thirsty souls who try to content ourselves with a picture of a glass of water, as opposed to the real thing. Stuck in familial and societal concepts of who we are, what we are, and what we should be doing, we are out of touch with our most fundamental needs.

At one point, when I was depressed, I was tempted to take antidepressants; but instead I prayed for help to understand the root of my suffering. Hours later, I was shown how I was living in concepts and fantasies of what a human being should be, based on images on television or in magazine and newspaper articles. Such facsimiles caused me to question everything about my life. How should I be? How should I look? What do others think of me? What movies should I watch? What people should I spend time with? My brain was on overload as I incessantly second-guessed my choices, including my choice of a spiritual path.

I didn't know how to be here, living day to day in a human body; I felt like an alien trying to figure out how to play the game. I would catch myself staring at people in cafés who seemed so normal and together and I wondered, "How do they manage to look so relaxed, spontaneous and polished?" Or I would turn on the television, and see Oprah Winfrey looking beautiful and conducting her show with ease, as she interviewed her talented guests. "How does she do that?" I wondered. I would also wonder how people made money in this world, and would invariably attract some New Age friends who had just completed a workshop that revealed the secret of how to become a millionaire. They would pontificate about my "poverty consciousness," while being poor as church mice themselves.

I didn't seem to fit in anywhere. Seeking a spiritual home, I couldn't find my place because many of the spiritual seekers whom I met would simply be parroting the words of a guru or master, as opposed to speaking from their own experience of God. Their words rang hollow, which left me feeling sad and lonely. Reading passages about living the pure spiritual life and the humility required, I'd feel that there was no hope for me because I had too much pride. I couldn't live up to how a "together" or a "spiritual" person should look, dress, speak or behave.

After sitting quietly for a while, I began to realize I was trying to find my source in fleeting concepts and attitudes. With my system clogged with empty words, nothing true could surface. Once I realized this, I could drop into a deeper place. Having faced the pain of my soul and my separation from the true Source, Love permeated my body, mind and spirit. I saw that everything in the external world is a concept; all we are is pure consciousness. My thirst to return to my Self was so strong that I had to meditate for many hours, drinking the nectar that came from inside and satiating every cell of my being. I saw how I had hurt myself in desiring to be something other than *who I really am*. I learned that my depression came from focusing my attention on the outer forms where no nourishment lies. Tears flowed from my eyes as the Divine water spilled out of me like an overflowing container of Love.

When we do not take the time to drink from within, we are always thirsty. And so we try to quench our thirst through overwork, sex, food, alcohol, surfing the Net, cigarettes, fantasies, drugs, etc. These are all escape mechanisms to keep us from facing our soul's innate yearning for The Divine in its many forms. Strip these obsessions away and we initially fall into despair. But the truth is that they will all be stripped away eventually, for they are all only concepts. When we draw our sustenance from the Self, from that which is eternal and fulfilling, our needs become simpler. False pictures lose their attraction.

When our car runs out of gas we must refuel, or the car will stop. We must also fill up with the fuel of the Self when we run low, or we will be unable to continue living in a balanced way. Instead we will turn to the outer concepts to fuel us, which can lead to addiction, greed, lust, anger, pride, fear, and hate. Love begins when we drink the true nectar of life, God's Love.

✤Meditation Keys – Concepts✤

Spend some quiet time witnessing one thing that is weighing heavily upon you. Let it reveal itself to you.

Pretend this heavy weight does not belong to you. Let it wash through you and leave your system. Do this until you become very still.

Watch the stillness fill you and reveal to you the Love that is who you really are.

Tug of Soul

I want so much to feel myself
But an overwhelming force tugs at me,
Telling me lies – making me do things I don't want to
do,
Making me smile when I want to turn away,
Making me feel unloved, unworthy, bound.
But I keep pretending and appearing to be okay,
Competent, together, when I don't feel it.
I have the Devil on one side and an Angel on the
other,
Both tugging at my soul,
As if they have nothing better to do than split me apart.
Why do I care so?
Who am I doing it for?
What do I think this game means?
Is there a winner or a loser?
Who is this me?
Could this game be but an illusion?
And is this me, really free?

Finding The True Face

Many years ago, I was lonely and joined a spiritual group (which I later realized was a cult) along with a couple of friends. The leader was trying to teach us to use our "spiritual" powers to manipulate and accumulate worldly things, such as wealth, romantic relationships, and so on. In her eyes, our spiritual progress was measured by how much we manifested in the world. My years of study and training and my own deeper knowing told me that Love was what mattered, not acquisitions, but I pushed all of that aside so I wouldn't be lonely any more. I did not judge what the leader was doing; I simply honored her extensive knowledge in the area of manifestation.

At one of our meetings, the leader allocated everyone to their original planet. I thought this was a hoot and I enjoyed laughing and having fun with the others in the group. The leader did not see what was so funny, however, and suggested to my friends that I had "psychic hooks" in them. My friends were so brainwashed by her and so entranced by her powers that they didn't see what was happening until much later. Having allowed myself to be vulnerable and open with everyone, I was devastated.

All I could do was roll up in a ball, trying to ease my aching heart. I prayed for understanding. After a while, I heard a distinct inner voice say, "Don't be afraid of losing face with people, there's nothing to worry about, you are divinely loved." A great sense of relief and strength swept over me and I recognize the gift of losing face, and the freedom that arises when I no longer care what others think of me. I then contemplated whether I was with my true knowing Self, who really knew my motivations, or was I trying to please others? I saw how I had given up my truth and had sold myself out in order to keep some friends. I had hid my true face.

Sometimes we're not even aware of how much energy we spend trying to be something other than *who we really are*. It is no wonder that confusion and destruction reign. As we try to unearth our true faces, we find ourselves trudging through a muddy swamp of old ways of being. We are wading through the games we've played to survive. It may seem as though we are retreating, not advancing.

Imagine that you have been living in a dark, dusty room for decades and have been okay with it. Then one day you decide to clean it up. Shining a light on the previously darkened room, you are shocked to discover that you have been living in mounds of debris, dust, and cobwebs. Just as we need to sweep away the cobwebs in the room, we need to sweep away those mental cobwebs that keep us from responding naturally to life in each moment. This is easier said than done.

We have a great need to be seen and acknowledged by others. The voice of our need for approval is often louder than the voice of our true Self. We all know what it is like to be judged by others; we have all experienced the desolation of losing face. When someone challenges our ego identity or false face, the one that has sold out in order to be loved, we feel abandoned. There is a gap between the true and natural self and the masks that we wear to survive. At the root of it lies fear, which tells us that we're not okay the way we are.

Upholding the false identity takes tremendous energy. The choice is clear. To open the door to our Divinity, we must honestly face ourselves and become humble before our true face, which is God.

✤Meditation Keys – Finding the True Face✤

✎ Reflect on a time when you have given yourself over to others in order to belong.

✎ Contemplate another time in your life when you have spoken your truth regardless of the outcome.

✎ How do they differ? In which would you prefer to live?

✎ Each day, choose one action to bring you closer to your true face.

Finding The True Face

The True Face	The Mask (The False Face)
✤ responds naturally without pretence.	✤ responds according to its perception of others' expectations.
✤ speaks the truth.	✤ speaks what it believes others want to hear.
✤ lives from the universal I.	✤ lives from the ego I.
✤ is internally motivated.	✤ is externally motivated.
✤ is not afraid to lose reputation or love.	✤ fears losing love, reputation, identity, because it feels love comes from external sources.
✤ knows love is infinite and cannot be lost.	✤ plays games and holds on tightly to everything, as it believes that love can be lost.
✤trusts intuitive feelings.	✤doubts intuitive feelings.
✤ is surrendered to God's will.	✤ fights God's will and believes what is perceived only with the eyes.

Unbinding the Prisoner

My hands grab and shake the prison bars.
"I want out of here. I've had enough", I scream.
The prison shrinks and closes in around me
Cutting off my life breath.
I scream out again but nobody hears me or even cares.
In fact, they're laughing at my ravings.
What are they laughing at? I need to know.
Then I look down and notice I am tying myself up
And binding my own arms.
I can't believe my eyes! I have taken myself prisoner.
I must be mad.
Then it occurs to me; if I can tie myself up,
I can free myself too.

The Only Way Out Is In

𝕴 have always wanted to move away from the city and its stress, noise, traffic and inordinately demanding people. But I have found that everywhere that I go, even far from town, I have encountered the same unwanted situations and personalities. It has seemed as though everyone, whether friends, family, or acquaintances, has needed my help or intervention. I have often found myself in situations where I have been called upon to act as counselor. Like broken records, people have needed to "share" their sad and hopeless stories, while never inquiring about my well-being. Even when I have chosen parts of town where they don't live, somehow they have found me only to dump their latest problem on me.

How could I escape? Tired of being the terminal sounding

board, I have made it clear that I need space, yet I would still get bombarded with phone calls from people with legitimate concerns, wanting only "a few moments of your time." Many clients have been unable to pay so I would work on a sliding scale that seemed always to slide to the low end; I felt as though I was working all the time with nothing to show for it. With declining health and financial resources, all I wanted was a home where I could meditate, take beautiful walks, and write. One day, while walking with a friend, I cried out to God, "Why can't I fulfil these simple desires? What do you want from me? I can't bear it any longer. I'm in prison." After a few minutes, an answer rose up from inside and my whole life appeared before me. I saw how all of these people were so familiar because they were part of me. I understood them because I knew their pain intimately, and whatever I resisted would appear in my life in the form of a friend or family member. I realized that this wasn't designed to imprison me but rather to expand my heart. At that point I stopped resisting and instead embraced each person as my own body and offered all of our problems to the Creator so that they might all be transmuted into love and peace.

As I continued to walk, a feeling of bliss welled up inside of me and I felt connected to everyone in my life as one body, one consciousness. The prison in which I had found myself was exactly what I needed to penetrate the nature of illusion. The real "I" was never imprisoned at all. The events of my life were designed to take me to oneness. I immediately felt free, calm, and centered. Without having shared a word about my experience, my friend suddenly turned to me and said, "God, you look different. Something big has changed in you."

Then I knew that the only way out is in.

We all live in a prison of sorts - the prison of our own minds that keeps unhappiness alive. The freedom to which we aspire will never be found outside ourselves. The freedom needs to be found within the prison itself, and only then do the walls dissolve. Otherwise, we go from country to country, therapist to therapist, relation-ship to relationship, striving for more money, more clothes, another diet, another love affair… Whatever we see and experience in the outer world is for only one purpose – to bring us back to the Divine Self. If we find ourselves becoming tired of the all-too-familiar patterns that become so amplified that we don't know where else to turn, we can consider ourselves lucky. The heat of transformation is on. The pressure is pushing on the walls of the prison - not to hurt us, but to free us and release us into the true Self. The only way out is in.

✣Meditation Keys – The Only Way Out is In✣

What is your particular prison? Where do you feel impris-oned in your life?

Spend some time contemplating what this sense of feeling imprisoned is teaching you.

What is the 'gift' that this imprisonment is giving to you?

The Fire of Love

More Love I cried. I need more Love.
I want Love to devour me and replace me
And leave nothing but the golden droplets of heaven.
My cry is heard – the fire begins.
It burns and burns.
I am left breathless at its fury.
Take it away! It hurts too much.
Let me go back to the cold waters of forgetfulness.
I don't have the courage I thought I had
And I don't understand what's happening.
But the fire rages.
And my resistance makes my pain even greater.
Golden flames rise higher and higher.
I, a smoke offering to God,
Finally, like a foundationless charred tree,
That can no longer hold up,
My shell crumbles to the ground.
Silence suddenly stills the air,
So deep- so dark -so rich.
Yet, there is one sound;
That of God's golden droplets
Falling from Heaven.

The Alchemist

Alchemy, or magic, occurs when the ordinary becomes extraordinary, when something apparently commonplace suddenly becomes luminous and profoundly alive. The conversion of the human perspective from mundane to golden could be compared to coal becoming diamonds. As we know, it takes considerable heat and pressure for such transformation to occur. In nature, all that grows has some kind of pressure or discomfort in it, as a new body, a new life is being birthed. This truth applies equally to the metamorphosis of human beings.

Jamie Sams and David Carson, authors of *Medicine Cards*, aptly describe this transformative process from the Native American perspective:

> "The transmutation of the life-death-rebirth cycle is exemplified by the shedding of Snake's skin. It is the energy of wholeness, cosmic

consciousness, and the ability to experience anything willingly and without resistance. It is the knowledge that all things are equal in creation, and that those things, which might be experienced as poison can be eaten, ingested, intergrated, and transmuted if one has the proper state of mind." (7)

As we emerge from the small self to become the master, magician, or alchemist, we may experience considerable mental, physical, and emotional discomfort. Learning to work with these pressures is the challenge. We can never judge God's work on us, however uncomfortable. We do not know what aspects of our personality or ego need to be burned away in order for us to shine like a flame of love. To become magical, we must love ourselves for who we are and for what is happening to us, aligning ourselves with our higher Self instead of fighting it. Then, when the pressures arise, we no longer see them as an irritation, but a Divine gift to teach us to hold love more deeply.

In his book, *The Prophet*, Kahlil Gibran, speaks to this:

"...For even as love crowns you, so shall he crucify you. Even as he is for your growth, so is he for your pruning. Even as he ascends to your height, and caresses your tenderest branches that quiver in the sun, So shall he descend to your roots and shake them in their clinging to the earth. Like sheaves of corn he gathers you unto himself. He threshes you to make you naked. He sifts you to free you from your husks. He grinds you to whiteness. He kneads you until

you are pliant; And then he assigns you to his
sacred fire, that you may become sacred bread
for God's sacred feast. All these things shall love
do unto you that you may know the secrets of
your heart, and in that knowledge become a
fragment of Life's heart." [8]

A magician sees everything in his/her world as an opportunity to fall into the heart and to drink the bliss of the
God Self.

Judgment, guilt, or a victim mentality, however, can
compound the suffering of Divine transformation, making the whole process seem like a misfortune. As we
enter into a higher frequency, we must embrace and
honor the pressure and the fire needed to remove the
dross. In each moment, there is a choice to indulge in
"poor me" thinking, or to accept these changes and
accompanying discomfort as a gift from our highest
Self. This kind of wisdom is what makes a true magician
or alchemist, as Kahlil Gibran tells us:

"...But if in your fear you would seek only love's
peace and love's pleasure, Then it is better for
you that you cover your nakedness and pass out
of love's threshing floor, into the seasonless
world where you shall laugh, but not all of your
laughter, and weep, but not all of your tears.
Love gives naught but itself and takes naught
but from itself. Love possesses not nor would it
be possessed; for love is sufficient unto love." [9]

Holding it all in the light, no matter how it looks, turns
the blazing fire into golden droplets of pure awareness

and bliss. Burning away our old beliefs, identities, and lifestyles will make room for a sacred human to be born.

✤Meditation Keys – The Alchemist✤

Imagine yourself as someone who has been chosen to birth a Love that is pure and true, and that will uplift many others.

Imagine you have also been given a warning that this Love does not birth without great challenges.

Contemplate whether or not you are ready for this initiation.

If you are, see yourself wholeheartedly accepting this mission with gratitude.

Know that your intention to move forward in this way will draw Grace into your life and you will be divinely guided.

Part

The
Door Closers

3

"When one door of happiness closes,
another opens;
but often we look so long at the closed door
that we do not see the one which has been opened for
us."

Helen Keller

The Being of Light from the far away galaxy looked again at the state of the humans on Earth and asked God, "How could they forget you and close the door to your infinite Love?"

God replied, "Naked and pure they roamed the earth's garden, tasting, smelling, touching, and hearing nothing but Love. Then one day, a slithering creature tempted them to eat the fruit of desire, promising them that they would then come to know good and evil and be as powerful as God. In their innocence, never having known anything but love, they ate the forbidden fruit. The creature then showed them that they were naked and therefore unworthy in the eyes of God. In shame, they ran to cover themselves, for in their simplicity, they believed what they were told. In that moment, their world of Love turned dark, and fear arose out of the darkness.

"I've done something wrong. I'm unworthy," they cried, running from the garden that was once their home. Desires arose that had not previously been there. Lust, greed, and pride took up residence in their hearts. They began to fight, to control, to hate, and to see each other as separate and frightening.

They learned to defend themselves and to protect their property from the threat of invasion from others. They created boundaries that no one could surmount. Duality and differences rose up among them. They believed that they were on their own, without the source of Love and divine protection that had always embraced them. Feeling profoundly empty, they overindulged the senses that had once been so refined, and their bodies became diseased. Greed ran rampant, as they tried to fill the hollowness inside; they began to destroy nature and each other in a vain attempt to have their needs met. To justify their cruelty and misuse of power, they also objectified one other.

They developed attachments to people and things that, when taken away, would give rise to untold suffering and loss. This would propel them back into the original pain of separation for which they would take drugs and alcohol to numb themselves. They became absorbed in being busy and in proving their intelligence to win others' approval. They became preoccupied with their thoughts. They strove to become worthy, believing that if they were truly good, God would love them.

Alternatively, they would act out their pain and anger attempting to attract God's attention that way. And so arose the sense of, "I am a good person"or "I am a bad person." This resulted in their having an increasing number of standards to live up to along with more shame and guilt if they somehow failed. The law of their world was called Karma – an eye for an eye, a tooth for a tooth – something that they had never known before because in the past they had known only oneness. Every time they performed a "wrong" action, they suffered tremendously in order to redress their misdemeanor. And they were rewarded for their "good" actions, but were never set free as this law of Karma was void of compassion and had them cycle forever, trapped in the prison known as birth and death. Their preoccupation with Karma would keep them from ever returning to me again and being as free as they had once been.

When they covered their nakedness, they covered their hearts and severed their pure connection to their eternal oneness and to the perfection of my garden. But the sensation of my Love, even though they had forgotten it, would haunt them their whole lives until they could no longer bear to be separate anymore. So their longing to return to my garden became the key that would eventually reunite us."

The EGO

Edging

God

Out

Have you ever wondered why, a short time after your spiritual experiences, you fall into a darkness that radically eclipses whatever light you may have experienced? Or have you noticed in an intimate relationship, that love and bliss are so available in the honeymoon stage but a few months or a year down the line, you find yourself in a power struggle and the bliss is out the window. Why is this?

Ego is the reason. Ego **E**dges **G**od **O**ut and darkens our light. All the saints and masters tell us that after the awakening stage we must make an effort to recognize ego when it arises and to begin to purify it as it blocks our connection to God.

Have you ever wondered why you have a mind-ego that separates you from God? Has it occurred to you that perhaps the negative tendencies that you encounter every day are not solely of your own making, but are in our atmosphere? Have you considered that perhaps the purpose of these dark energies is to keep us separate from God? If everything is God, why is the voice of the inner Self so difficult to hear?

These questions have always plagued me. I have found that they have never been fully answered in most scriptures that I've studied. I have always struggled with the mind that seemed for some reason to be stronger and louder than the voice of the inner Self. I would fight hard for the Truth because deep inside I would know *who I really am* but sometimes it felt like a losing battle. I have even felt that God had made a big mistake and that this kind of struggle in which we all engage is not right.

As though in response to my quandary, I met Sant Rajinder Singh Ji Maharaj, who lives his life in an egoless state. Upon meeting him, I experienced great joy and beauty, which I hadn't felt for a long time. The gentleness that emanated from him was so heartwarming and so luminous that all I could do was cry as my hardened sense of rebellion dissolved. It was not anything he said. I simply witnessed the contrast between his humility and my pride. But I also cried because my soul was filled with the love of God in a subtle yet profound way.

In response to the question, "How is the mind the root cause of placing layers on the soul?" Sant Rajinder says:

"When the mind is driven by its desires, it can

overpower the subtle soul. One would think
soul, with its infinite power, could be strong and
resistant, but the nature of the world is such that
the mind is operating in its home territory. The
situation is similar to two basketball teams in the
playoffs. The team playing in its home city has
the home court advantage. The crowds are
cheering for this team, which is comfortable in
its own environment. Similarly, the mind is at
home in the world. The soul is but a guest visit-
ing temporarily. The mind has the advantage in
this world of matter, whereas the soul is out
of its element here. The mind's desires lead it
into an array of situations to get what it wants.
It will stop at nothing in the pursuit of fulfilling
its wants and needs." [10]

So we can see that there is a great battle being waged
between mind and soul. But why do we need to be in a
battle? If everything is God, why is the soul not in its
home territory? Kabir, another great saint, born in the
14th century, speaks about the origin of Creation in *The
Anurag Sagar of Kabir*. There he outlines how, in the
beginning, the original God, Sat Purush, created sixteen
sons, one of whom, Kal, was unable to handle the separation from his father that the process of Creation
demanded. Thus Kal went mad and misused the tools of
Creation entrusted to him, creating "a sewer where a
garden was intended." [11] "Kal" literally means, "Time"
or "Darkness." [12] It is the name of the Negative Power,
or that aspect of the One God that flows downward and
is responsible for the creation and maintenance of the
causal, astral and physical worlds. A very large part of
Anurag Sagar is concerned with Kal's fall from grace and

favor through demanding the sovereignty of these three worlds. Kal sends his incarnations into the world from time to time to maintain justice and redress wrongs, but also to mislead seeking souls and prevent them from leaving the confines of the three worlds.

Kal is not necessarily evil. A careful reading of the *Anurag Sagar* indicates that he has an essential role in the lower creation. However Kal is not good either, although he demands to be worshipped as though he were God. Because he does his best to keep individual souls from leaving the lower creation, he is the ancient foe of the Saints, or incarnations of Sat Purush, whose work is precisely to help souls leave the lower creation. In the Jewish-Christian tradition, Kal is in some ways comparable to Satan. He is also analogous to the "priestly" conception of Yahweh in the Old Testament (although not to the prophetic use of Yahweh, which refers to a God of mercy and love). The Gnostics called Kal the Demiurge, and understood him very well. Perhaps the closest Kal archetype in Western literature is William Blake's Urizen who, like Kal, functions as the great lawgiver, using his laws to trap humanity, and demanding to be worshipped as God. Although Kal is often referred to in *Anurag Sagar* as "unjust," that is from the perspective of the Sat Purush and Kabir. Within the context of the worlds that Kal created, he was absolutely fair and just, demanding and getting "an eye for an eye and a tooth for a tooth." Within Kal's framework, we cannot avoid sin. Thus, it is true that we get exactly what we deserve according to the Law of Karma. But since the ultimate Reality of the human condition is that we are children of the Sat Purush, "drops of His essence," Kal, seen from that perspective, prevents us from realizing our full Divinity and thus is monstrously unjust. Our mind is related to Kal in the same way that our soul is related to Sat Purush, the Supreme God. [11]

During the period that I was writing this section of the book, I was meditating one morning and, as I began to focus inward, all manner of thoughts arose. I would become still and then I'd remember something I had to buy that day. I'd pull my attention back to my center and, in a flash, I'd be daydreaming about some Hawaiian tropical paradise. I'd bring myself back from Hawaii only to find myself in Toronto with my ailing mother. My attention would flit from one thing to the next – my health, my sore foot, the noise from the traffic outside, the dogs barking... The clock continued to tick and finally the alarm went off signaling the end of my " meditation." I was meditating on the mind or the world of form, rather than the soul or the source of all life. That morning, the mind was showing me its power and how it can so easily pull us away from our soul in this physical realm that we live in. That meditation is an example of how so many of us keep cycling round and round in a sea of thoughts never free enough to know *who we truly are*. We are also trapped by our desires, which are louder than the soul's gentle voice. Wherever the mind puts its focus, the soul has to follow. Hence our soul starves and is left hungry for true nourishment that comes only from placing our attention within. According to Sant Rajinder Singh, "As the mind runs amok in its home court, it gets embroiled in the five deadly passions: anger, lust, greed, attachment, and ego. Each time we succumb to the mind's desires, more layers block our brilliant soul. " [13]

We can tell what team we are on by noticing if we are coming from the soul, a place of love, or if we are coming from the mind/ego, a place of pride, lust, greed, fear, etc. This practice of "witnessing" – determining where we are placing our attention – is an awesome task, which is why saints like Kabir stressed the need for a Master who could help pull us from the world of the mind to the world of the soul.

How does the mind close the door to the soul? The answer lies in the nature of mind, which continually thinks and dwells on whatever arises. Because of our conditioning, the mind's focus or attention is always drawn to the distractions of the outer world. Thus we get further and further away from experiencing the bliss that comes from connecting with our soul. The ego is always identifying itself with the things projecting a sense of "I" or "mine." According to Swami Muktananda, the great Siddha Yoga Master,

> "The mind and ego are not two different things. In fact, the mind, the intellect, the memory and the ego are only different aspects of one faculty…the inner mind…These four aspects are vital to the human being. They intervene between the senses and the Self. They make communication between the Spirit and the senses possible… The ego is a very bad enemy. It converts heaven into hell. It has reduced the Divine Being into a bound creature. It is the ego which sees the impure in the pure and which forces man to undergo all sorts of suffering and misery. It is the ego that causes a separate existence." [14]

How does the mind/ego create a separate existence? Thoughts are floating around us constantly, many of them not even ours. It is what we do with these thoughts that will create either a heaven or a hell. If we put all of our focus on form, we will create hell for ourselves, because everything will eventually die or go away and we will suffer in emptiness. If we place our focus on our inner Self, we will create heaven, because we will touch eternity which never dies or goes away; we will realize our oneness with God.

So how do we edge God out? The voice of the ego is powerful, highly charged, and speaks with much conviction. Wherever there is separation, duality or differences, there is ego. Living a life from the perspective of ego is living and believing we are the body alone, and that our survival and well-being depend entirely upon the fulfillment of the body's desires, actions, feelings, and thoughts. We edge God out by believing that we are the doers of all action, and that we must fulfill our desires at all costs. Such a belief keeps the door closed to the voice of the soul, which is always trying to lead us back to the love of God. God's love is available in every moment, but in the realm of ego the mind is so prevalent and pulls at us so unrelentingly, that few people avail themselves of this gift.

Instead, we plod along doing the best we can, trying to fit into roles that are constricting, not unlike shoes that don't fit. They hurt and so do we. We worry that our needs won't get met. Our fear creates greed and we take what isn't ours, because of the illusion that there isn't enough to go around. When it appears as if we have accomplished something great, we are fueled by pride and arrogance. Then, we become self-righteous because we think we know all the answers. Because of our limited understanding, we are patronizing and condescending to others. We judge them for their differences; we try to fit them into our own boxes, so we don't have to face our own fears and limitations. We fear death because we don't know what it holds for us. We resist our lives, because they are neither pleasant nor satisfying without the connection to our soul – and our soul continually haunts us. No matter what desires we fulfill or what accomplishments we achieve in this world, we are without peace.

The ego believes itself to be the truth. The ego believes that the passing thoughts and feelings are real. My thoughts. My feelings. My opinions. My house. My child. These impressions build up over long periods of time and an apparently solid belief about reality is formed. The ego also carries the energy of excitement; thus, we often feel energized by our identities, even if they are destructive.

Many of us feel it is healthy to have an ego. After all, how would we survive without one? But being free from ego is a life of true beauty that will never arise from our driving and striving. Freedom from ego can only occur when the foundation of our lives is based on the pure "I," or the "I" that is not separate from others, the "I" that knows and sees only Love, the "I" that is one with God. This "I" can only be experienced when we pierce the ego, the small self that thinks it has a separate existence. Only then can we see our ego as the albatross that we carry around our necks, which serves no purpose other than to weigh us down and keep us angry, prideful, and separate.

In the world of ego, everything is based on good and bad, right and wrong, and duality of every kind. We fight and judge our feelings trying to make them happy ones. This is comparable to moving the furniture around from one side of the room to the other; nothing really changes. We spend all of our time identifying with every thought to make it real and solid, leaving no time for the crying soul.

Our God Self is the unchanging reality. When we turn to The Divine for what is real and true, the magic doorway opens to show us that we've never been good or bad, right or wrong, happy or sad. We have only been trying on costumes; we have mistaken them for reality only to fall prey to an infectious disease. This disease has many symptoms: hatred, defensiveness, greed, pride, lust, prejudice, resistance, guilt, doubt, impatience, judgment, self-righteousness, anger, resentment, jealousy, unworthiness... All of these symptoms are based on fear (**f**alse **e**vidence **a**ppearing **r**eal).

So, what is real (**r**ight **e**vidence, **a**ll **l**ove)? In the coming pages, we will explore the states that arise from our exclusive identification with being a body and/or personality. We will work with poems that amplify the impact of each of these states. Thus, we will witness the struggle between soul and mind and we will begin to recognize how we keep the door closed to the divine Self.

What is the key to open this door? The answer is, *Love for ourselves and all others* who are caught in the grips of these symptoms. Just as parents love their children when they are ill, we need to love ourselves and each other as we heal from the illness of separation from

God. *Having the intention to bring all of our experiences to the feet of God is the key.* Every ego quality is but another reminder to return to God's Love.

I Must Have It

*Oh how my heart is aching and beating
And all of my senses are reaching out
To devour and merge with this object that I so desire
I must have it, for my life depends upon it
I know that it will fill all of my needs
And make me forever at peace
You're telling me that I'm deluded?
And that desire is a bottomless pit of empty promises?
No! Please just let me have this one thing
Then I'll listen to you, I promise
I really need this object of my desire
As it will be the fulfillment of all of my hopes and
dreams
You want me to surrender to God – the creator of all
objects?
Yes, I'll do that later, if you just help me with this one
last thing
If I can't have it I know I will die
And if you refuse to help me, then please close that
door when you leave.*

DESIRE

Life contains but two tragedies, one is not to get your heart's desire the other is to get it.

Oscar Wilde

esire could be characterized as the original sin that we all carry within our genes. We desire more money, a better car, a bigger house, a more satisfying career, recognition, love, good relationships, a slimmer or more youthful body... The list goes on and on. Our whole life is based on fulfilling one desire or another.

There was a time when I longed for a home in a quiet neighborhood, close to everything. I would look in the newspapers and on the Internet at listings of houses for sale, none of which I could afford. I would walk the streets, looking into people's back yards, trying to imagine what it would be like to sit on a quiet back deck with just my own thoughts instead of the clamour of the crowded apartment building where I lived. This desire became so strong that I could think of nothing else but finding a home to rest in. But it was financially impossible. I was grief-stricken that I would have to live the rest of my life without peace and quiet. Then I became angry that I had focused so much of my earlier life on spirituality, that every penny had been spent on searching for deeper meaning and not on accumulating wealth. The anger became sadness as I reflected on how little I had to show for my life materially. One day, as I was walking by multimillion-dollar properties in one of the wealthiest areas of town, the pain of being unable to purchase a home became very acute. I couldn't bear it a moment longer and I sat down on a bench and cried in anguish. "I will die if I can't have a home to rest in," I thought, and I truly believed it. But then, a tiny little flash of light shot through my thoughts and I realized, "I am putting all of my energy into desiring and leaving nothing for my life and my soul!" This awareness shook me out of my grieving. I woke up to how ephemeral life is; a peaceful home will not protect me from death. I placed myself in the home of my dreams, and imagined living my life from there. Fundamentally, there would not be much difference from my current life. I would still need to get up, exercise, meditate, cook, clean, eat, work, sleep, garden, etc. I realized that, ultimately, the amount of time that I could actually enjoy the house would be minimal.

I began to look at the nature of desire itself, to try and understand the incredible power that it had over me. The only way out of my dilemma was to capture desire itself before it grabbed onto those thoughts that said, "House, home, rest, peace." To avoid creating a painful reality for myself, I needed to take the focus off of desiring objects; I needed to look at desire as a form of God arising from consciousness. I would then be able to witness my desire from a place of awareness rather than chasing after it and being disappointed. Without the object of house/home, the desire I felt turned into, "I Am." "I am one with God, I already have everything I need," reverberated inside of me. It's at times like these that my original spiritual awakening experience returns to remind me of *who I really am.*

The realization, "I am God" arose from desire without attachment to an object, which again showed me that nothing exists that is not God. In the *Vijnana Bhairava*, a scripture of Kashmir Shaivism, Dharana #75 speaks about this experience:

> "When a desire or knowledge (or activity) appears, the aspirant should, with mind withdrawn from all objects (of desire, knowledge, etc.), fix his mind on it (desire, knowledge, etc.) as the very Self. Then he will have the realization of the essential Reality." [15]

My experience with desiring a home humbled me into having greater compassion for all of us who suffer the pain and disappointment that comes from unmet desires. *The antidote to desire, then, is to shift our attention from the object(s) of desire to desire itself, and then to experience desire as God within.* From that place, we can know that what is ours will come to us without asking.

✦Meditation Keys – Desire✦

🗝 *Recall a time when you experienced intense desire for something or someone.*

🗝 *Allow yourself to feel this desire as fully as possible.*

🗝 *Now, take the object of desire away and let yourself feel the energy of desire itself.*

🗝 *Feel the sensation of desire fully within you. Having withdrawn your focus from without to within, feel the burning desire with your whole being.*

🗝 *Know that what you are feeling is in fact God's desire for you.*

🗝 *Use this as an opportunity to melt into the fire of God's desire for you.*

🗝 *Recognize that God knows all of your desires and relax into acceptance of whatever is being presented to you in this moment.*

DESIRE

* Desire is the source of all separation.
* Desire creates great anger when it is not fulfilled.
* Desire is at the root of greed, lust, attachment, pride and even fear.
* Desire is the emperor of the negative power as it controls us so completely.

I Need More

I need more
I have not the time to wait, to listen to some voice that
I can barely hear
I have desire and I will fulfill it
Don't stand in my way
You're telling me I'm actually looking for God's love?
And you say that's why I'm acting greedy and
aggressive?
Ridiculous!
Now you're saying that that's also why I'm lustful and
full of pride
Go away – I don't want to hear your talk about love
Love doesn't look after me – taking what I want looks
after me
My greed feeds me
My lust satiates me
My pride lets me feel worthy
I need no one
You say that God can only be heard with quiet, humble
ears, free of the need for praise
Well, my ears have lots of need for praise
My eyes have lots of need for gold
My mouth wants to taste the finest delights
So, perhaps you will have to look elsewhere for
another candidate to offer this divine elixir
you speak about
I must close the door now and say goodbye

Greed

reed begins with the thought, "I am not enough," and then escalates to a compulsion for more things – more money, more food, more sex, more people, more recognition... "More! More! More!" is the mantra of greed. Looking at our greed with compassion, we can see our starved souls, desperately trying to fill themselves with whatever they can. But in our efforts to fill ourselves up, we are barking up the wrong tree. According to Swami Anantananda, a monk in the Siddha Yoga tradition,

> "Greed's only measure of satisfaction is the sensation of having obtained more. More is an attribute of comparison. So the moment we acquire something and experience it as having the quality of being more than we had before, there is a sense of satisfaction. However, that sensation, like all sensations, quickly fades. Then what we have no longer feels like more; it is just what we have. So greed sets in again.

This cycle is endless. In it, no actual amount of anything will ever be enough." (16)

We have all been greedy on occasion, usually when we are most afraid of not having our needs met. When I have felt greedy, it has been at times when I didn't think that I have enough money or love to survive. Greed always arises from fear. I'm sure that many crimes that are committed in our world come from a survival fear of one kind or another. How many white-collar crimes are committed because of greed? Executives at major corporations such as WorldCom or Enron have risked their personal reputations and lost everything because of having been captured by greed. But if we were to probe for the real motivation behind these crimes, we would likely find that some deep fear was the true cause. Perhaps they fell prey to another belief at the heart of greed, "There is not enough to go around."

When we are in the state of greed, it is very difficult to break free of it and to return to the soul who knows that God takes care of all of us. We are paralyzed by the fear that we won't be cared for unless we push or manipulate things and people in order to get what we need. But greed is a disease that can never be fulfilled as it sees only lack and therefore takes. The soul, on the other hand, sees only fullness and naturally wants to give. That is why the soul and greed have a hard time co-existing.

What is the antidote for greed? It is being grateful for what we have, knowing that we are enough as we are and that we have enough, and having the generosity to share this abundance with others. We must also exercise vigilance in order to capture greed before it grabs hold of a desire.

✤Meditation Keys – Greed✤

🔑 *Recall a time when you have felt greedy.*

🔑 *Allow yourself to feel those sensations now. What thoughts emerge from this state of greed? What feelings do these thoughts give rise to?*

🔑 *Now recall a time in which you have freely given with no conditions.*

🔑 *Allow yourself to feel the sensations emerging from your generosity. What thoughts does this state of giving give rise to? What feelings do these thoughts give rise to?*

🔑 *When do you feel closest to your God self?*

🔑 *Next time that you experience greed arising in you, STOP before it takes hold and do something generous immediately.*

GREED

* Greed believes that we are separate and must take from others to fill the Self.
* Greed starts small and almost imperceptibly. Then, it grows like a weed that wraps around and chokes the beauty out of everything.
* Greed runs rampant in the world today and in ourselves. More, more; better, better; different, different are greed's cries.
* Greed's voice is louder than the voice of truth, so it seems to have more power.
* Greed laughs at God's plans for us and the patience required for our soul's unfolding.

I am Right

I am only doing this for your own good.
It's because I love you that I am concerned.
I know what is best for you.
The way you are is wrong.
The way you think is wrong.
You must change and come over to my way of thinking.
I know what's right – you unfortunately don't.
You must fit into this world I am making for you.
Differences are not acceptable here.
Don't turn away – you will be sorry.
Look at how well I live.
People respect me.
I have a good position – you have nothing,
But this strange hunger for something nobody can see.
You are a failure – a nobody.
Don't tell me we're all nothing but parts of God.
I won't believe it.
If you can't see it, how can it be real?
Are you telling me that I live in a solid prison of walls?
Where do you live?
In some unseen realm in the sky, going nowhere?
At least I know where I stand.
I'm on this side of the door.

Self-righteousness And Judgement

Self-righteousness and judgement arise from the ego identity, "I am right." Adolph Hitler, the Nazi leader who ordered the annihilation of countless Jews during the Second World War, took this belief to its darkest extreme. Using his power and charisma, he presented an image of the superiority of the Aryan race that was so persuasive that prejudice and hatred toward non-Aryan people ran rampant.

The Hitler story is an amplified form of self-righteousness. But it shows clearly just how this disease can easily destroy all that is good. When we examine our own lives, many of us can see where we've been self-righteous with our partners, children, parents, friends or co-workers. Sometimes our self-righteousness comes from truly wanting the best for those we love. For example, we want our children to make life choices that will make them happy. However, in wanting them to be safe and well, we can tend to guide them from a place of mild disrespect based on fear, not really honoring their own understanding. Of course the children rebel because we've distanced ourselves from them and haven't tried to find out what is dear to them and what might bring out their receptivity.

Mistreating a store clerk or gas station attendant for what we consider to be poor service is an all-too-common example of unconscious self-righteousness. I once was involved with a wealthy man who was wonderful in many ways, but every time he dealt with a maid, employee, waiter, or anyone without money or prestige, he would become overbearing and rude. He would even try to teach them how to do their job properly as if they had just arrived on the planet with no life experience. I felt heartsick seeing these people walking away feeling small and disempowered, but when I questioned him on his behavior, he didn't even realize that he was doing it! He was just responding and behaving according to what he had learned from his parents. This showed me that self-righteousness can be an unconscious, learned behavior.

If we are honest with ourselves, we can see numerous ways in which we separate ourselves from others by believing that we are right and they are wrong. *What is the antidote that will open the closed door of self-righteousness and judgement? It is equality and compassion. It is seeing each person that comes before us as another manifestation of God with a gift of beauty and uniqueness.*

Self-righteousness cannot survive in the midst of appreciation and oneness with all others. The key is to capture self-righteousness and judgmental behavior before it is projected onto others.

When we see the God Self reflected in all others, we immerse ourselves in God's Love and self-righteousness dissolves. God's Love dissolves all fear and where there is no fear, there is no judgement.

✤Meditation Keys – Self-righteousness and Judgement✤

Recall a time in which you have judged someone (or when someone whom you trust has told you that you were being judgmental) and believed that you were right.

How did this state of judgement make you feel? Did it bring you closer to the person you were judging, or did it distance you from them? What did you learn from this encounter?

If it distanced you, visualize the same situation being replayed, only this time put your "I am right" aside.

Now listen to the point of view of the person toward whom you were being judgmental, as if it contained a great gift for you.

Imagine yourself giving your point of view in response, while seeing both perspectives as shimmering aspects of a multifaceted diamond.

See the validity of both perspectives and ask the Higher Power for the solution that will empower and uplift everyone.

SELF-RIGHTEOUSNESS AND JUDGEMENT

* Self-righteousness hides unworthiness, pride and fear in a box of false knowledge and separation.
* Self-righteousness believes that it knows the right way to do things and judges anyone or anything that is different.
* Self-righteousness has to prove that it is right in order to keep its powerful stance intact.
* Self-righteousness must judge so that it can separate itself from others to keep its power.
* Self-righteousness needs to cultivate an "us" and "them" kind of thinking which then makes it easier to judge and condemn.
* Self-righteousness is fearful of ever acknowledging or appreciating the beauty and uniqueness of others because this would dissolve its identification with "I am right," thus melting its hard outer shell.

I am Special

I will show no weakness
They don't deserve me
It's just a role you say I'm playing, it's not really who
I am?
Well this role that I play is important and worthy
And I am separate from you
Better than you
Smarter than you
I am more special than the others
So don't ask me to open myself up to you
Who are you to ask me to come down from my
pedestal?
Why should I? It's safe here
It's solid here
Where you live is too vulnerable
Oh so you think that it's too real and too frightening
for me
Well I am too smart to let myself fall into the abyss of
nothingness
I think that you pray to God because you are weak
Where does it get you?
You dare to tell me that I need to let go of control
in order to experience love?
Why? I am powerful. I have all the love I need.
I create my own reality and I need nothing else.
What control or power do you have?

Some esoteric belief in peace in the moment?
Go away – I will not become one with all of those
other people
I'd rather die than become lost in your ocean of humility
Where everyone becomes the same -
Boring, weak and unimportant
I know I'm right here so just close the door
as you leave.

Pride

Pride hardens distinctions, draws lines, and then goes to war to sustain them; humility lets them go.

Swami Anantananda

𝕴 have a special relationship with a friend whom I've known for many years. Sometimes we get together and have a good laugh about clothes we used to wear to show off, or about identities that we had assumed and truly believed ourselves to be, or about how vain and full of pride we had been – about nothing. She had always wanted to be a world-famous healer but as she has matured, her pride has been tempered somewhat. She has become more of a recluse than a famous person. I too had wanted to be "seen" and to contribute great things but now I am more inclined to run from anything that tries to pull me into engagement with the world. For both my friend and I, our pride was more obvious at one point and, through a process of purification, has become more subtle. However it is still deeply embedded in us and is difficult to identify much of the time. It has not gone away. Pride is synonymous with ego. Just as ego grabs all the thoughts that pass by and identifies with them, pride will grab anything to be proud of, whether it is admirable or not. Pride is not particular as long as it can show off. How many times in the course of even one day, does our pride rear its head and show off somehow, even if only in a small way? Often, we don't even notice. The pain from all of those times that we weren't seen or acknowledged as a child still follows us around looking for that pat on the back from our adult peers. Most people can't wait to tell their story and be the center of attention. We all want to be viewed in a favourable light, which is why we strive so hard to attain money, power, good looks – all the things that we believe will be admired and recognized by others.

In our world we have a fascination with egos that seem to be able to do it all, seemingly without help. We confuse strength with ego, and vulnerability with weakness. We don't understand humility as so few people have it. Pride lives everywhere. Consider how much we care about what others think of us: "How do I look?" "What are they thinking about what I just said?" or "I will not reveal my true feelings in case they judge me or think less of me." Think about how embarrassing it is to make a mistake or how difficult it is to stand up for what our heart feels, for fear of appearing too vulnerable or weak. We prefer to keep up the good false image, rather than shed a tear of truth.

Our need to hide from others and be right arises from a belief that we are separate from the God Self and from others. This, in turn, gives rise to fear, pride, and defensiveness. We don't realize that when we indulge our pride we only hide from ourselves and reinforce the belief that there is someone outside of us upon whose good opinion we are dependent. As long as we believe we are separate from the God Self and others, there will be someone for whom to show off, someone to fear, and someone from whom we stay distant.

Whenever we feel that something is wrong with us or with our lives, we invite turmoil and struggle. When we touch that place within that trusts that a higher power is truly in control, we let go of struggle, enjoy the moment, and silently slip into our divinity. Otherwise, we are impatient, angry, self-righteous, depressed, dissatisfied, and anxious – cut off from the source of Love. Instead of hiding out in pride, we must move through the door of acceptance so that Love can pour through.

In our hurried lives, we often feel that if we wait for the help of God, whatever we want to accomplish won't get done, so we attempt to do it alone. "I did it," is the root of pride. Including God in every activity, every need, every thought, every feeling, is the greatest door opener to our divine Self. The "I" that refers to the body and the body's needs and activities is small, limited, and ego-driven. The "I" that speaks of ourselves as a universal being, completely connected to all of life and others, is the "I" with whom we wish to identify ourselves. In the latter "I" is great humility; the former "I" speaks of separation and ego.

According to Swami Anantananda, "Pride is about comparisons made in forgetfulness." We are all singular human beings with many qualities that are unique to us;

but we forget that we are all a part of God, not separate as pride would have us believe. Siddha teacher Swami Muktananda used to tell a story, *The Lords' Club*, in which all members were children of lords. In order for the club to function, they all took turns fulfilling the different roles – from footman to cook to president. However, they never forgot that they were all children of lords and therefore equals. In telling this story, Muktananda would conclude, "No matter what work we are doing, we are all children of the Lord. This world is the Lord's club. No matter what position we hold, our awareness of being the Lord should never change. The supreme Truth is within every person...A person should not think, 'I am this,' or 'I am that.' These kinds of feelings are transitory. They are short-lived. When you are playing a certain role, you have a certain name, but it is not the ultimate Truth." [17]

Pride is everywhere and keeps us away from our true Self by trying to keep us believing that we're separate from God. Kabir, the great Indian saint-poet of the 15th century, said that pride is as hard to see as a black ant in a dense forest on a moonless night.[18] It can seem impossible to detect our pride as it is so all-pervasive and interwoven throughout our whole being.

As I was contemplating this section of the book, I had a moment of clarity in which I could see the extent to which pride rules and motivates my life. It was a humbling realization because I knew that out of my own strength I could not stop it. This became evident after observing my pride all day and trying to change my behavior in situations where I might want to show off, or seek others' admiration for my intelligence, knowledge, and so on. But I soon discovered that pride ran much more deeply than just my behaviour; it formed my identity. I also saw that pride is a cry for love and in fact could be characterized as *love gone wrong*. In our every action, conscious or unconscious, we are looking for love, no matter how our behaviour may appear to others. We are often so frustrated and so in need of love that we will sell our soul to the devil for a word of approval from another. Pride is everyone's cry for love, but our cry will never be heard if we seek fulfillment in the external world. Our cries will be heard only when we turn our face to God, which is the source of all Love. *What is the antidote to pride? Admitting our powerlessness in the face of pride's immensity and, with humility and gratitude, speaking from the heart and asking for God's help, knowing that we are unable to break free on our own.* We must try and capture pride itself before it tries to grab hold of something to be proud of.

✣Meditation Keys – Pride✣

🔑 As if you were a scientist, spend a day observing yourself in your interactions with others and notice when your pride looms up. Notice occasions in which you try to be seen or acknowledged by others. Notice those times in which you try to be better or even less than others. Make no judgments. Just notice.

🔑 Pick another day, and observe the people in your life more closely. Notice occasions in which their pride looms up. Make no judgments. Just notice.

🔑 Just as a scientist would be grateful when making discoveries, feel the gratitude for having discovered this disease called pride permeating the human race.

🔑 With great compassion, offer the pain of this disease to God. Ask that we all may be blessed with Divine Love so that our craving for temporary approval becomes longing for the eternal.

PRIDE

* Pride fears vulnerability, as it would destroy its power.
* Pride believes that it creates its own reality and doesn't need God's intervention.
* Pride uses any opportunity to show off its intelligence, its physical beauty, its creativity, and its accomplishments, even its spiritual evolution.
* Pride's favorite word is "me."
* Pride will claim anything to be proud of, even poverty and illness.
* Pride wants to be different and look better than whatever it encounters.

It's not me, It's you

I feel fine
I feel sorry for you guys
Quit holding that mirror in front of my face
You say that I must let go of judging, berating and
blaming you
For who you are and what you do
I wouldn't say it if it wasn't true
You are wrong
You want me to take responsibility for my projection?
Well your way feels like work that I don't want to do
After all, this problem is your fault
And I don't remember inviting you here
Are you trying to tell me that you and I are one?
I can't take anymore of your relentless torture
You're mad
Get out of here…and close that door behind you

Blame

Blame is one of the greatest door closers to our divine connection. When we blame someone or something, we are affirming our separation from the source of life. We are affirming that we are alone, and that our own God Self does not exist.

A wise teacher, Shirley Luthman, whom I studied with for a few years, was a master of human and Divine nature. She said that nobody could do anything to you that you were not already doing to yourself. When I heard this, I was shocked into the realization that there is nobody "out there." It seemed so much easier to blame others and to be separate than to take responsibility for my reality. This teaching felt like a bitter pill to swallow. It meant that everyone was "me." Everyone was wearing the perfect costume for me to learn about myself and the collective consciousness that we share. Shirley taught me that these disguises are the illusions that we must learn to see through in order to know

God. Her work was remarkable in bringing many people to the understanding that we are nothing but Love and that we are all of the same body, so who then is there to blame? I could no longer rest as a victim of people or circumstances. I had to be fully accountable for my own experience.

While reflecting on this essay, I had a conversation with a friend about the nature of blame. He noted the all-pervasiveness of blame and how it, like pride, reinforces the separation from God. Blame is so universally ingrained in us that we create agreements with others that certain things and people must be blamed – the taxman, the politician, the crooked organizations… In our more intimate interactions with friends or family members, we can obtain support to blame our partners or our children for our troubles. Many of us blame our parents for our shortcomings and we habitually blame others when we are hurt. People sue one another because of blame and people kill because of blame; the list is endless.

In these moments of blame, we have forgotten that this world is a reflection of our own consciousness. We have forgotten that we are one with everything. We see people as separate and different and because they are separate, they can have power over us, or us over them. This game is like looking in the mirror to fix our hair, but instead of reaching for our own hair, we try to rearrange the hair in our reflection. We must always return to the Source because the perception rests with us, no one else. God, Life, Inner Self – all of these things are Love. And Love only wants to evolve back to its Source. Anywhere we believe we are separate, someone or something will be staring at us to confirm it. We tend to blame them for our painful reflections, yet when we hold anyone in a place of separation, even the taxman or the government, we keep our door forever closed.

We must understand that those things, people, and situations that carry a negative charge for us reflect a part of us that needs to be deeply contemplated and loved. This is essential so we can learn that whatever it is that we continually blame, is in fact a gift from God to help show us that Love permeates everything. When we drop blame, Love remains.

What is the antidote to blame? Letting go of feeling that we are victims of circumstance and recognizing that there is a purpose and perfection for everyone and everything in our lives. There are no accidents. When we see everything and everybody as one body of God, even the so-called negative power has within it the unbearable pressure that can ultimately drive us back to ourselves. The art is to capture the energy of blame before it separates and is projected onto another.

Meditation Keys – Blame

Choose an "impossible" person whom you blame for your unhappiness. Get a piece of paper, place his or her name at the top of it, and list everything that you hate about this person. Give yourself complete freedom. Blame him or her as much as you want to.

Now, look at your list and replace his or her name with your name. How are you similar to this person? Contemplate this.

BLAME

* Blame takes no responsibility for itself, but projects anything that we want to disown about ourselves onto another person, country, race, religion, politician, etc.
* Blame creates war because it separates us so that we can make our enemies wrong and then kill them.
* Blame believes that it is a victim of something or of someone else's actions.
* Blame is a protection from feeling our vulnerability.
* Blame has no compassion for itself or others, which is why it can be hurtful.
* Blame will hurt itself, if it can't find someone or something else to focus on.
* Blame does not like looking in the mirror.

So are You

Oh, the day is sunny
I'm so happy, and so are you.
Oh, the day is so grim.
I am so miserable, and so are you
Oh, the stars and the heavens bring joy to my senses
And so, too, to yours
Oh, the moon is covered by a black ominous hue
So it must be true for you too
Oh, wild I am,
Rich I am,
And powerful too.
Funny, I see the same things in you.
A demon has grabbed my soul and my money
And left me without a clue.
Why are you so sad – what's wrong with you?
Who are you anyway?
You follow me around
Whatever I am feeling – there you are like a hound
Like an actor, you keep coming around
Looking back at me in all my friends, my family
And even in my own town.
Who are you? Who am I?
This is all too confusing,
I need to close this door so I can figure all this out.

Projection

rejection is a powerful tool used unconsciously in a world seen in only one dimension. Since we view the world only through our own perspective, everything appears to be dancing in front of us, reflecting the way we feel in that moment. Imagine times in which you've gone on holiday. Feeling happy and free, you meet someone special. The place itself is exceptionally beautiful. You feel wonderful inside – satisfied and happy. The world appears magical as if in that moment, time itself has stopped. The next year you return to the same place for another holiday. Maybe you're alone this time, or you've lost your job. Perhaps your health isn't great. You look at the scenery and it's a nice view – but the magic has gone. What happened? Same spot; different experience.

The same thing happens with the people in our lives, whether they're close friends, family, casual acquaintances, or people we encounter on the street. We label them according to the impressions and sensations we are experiencing in the moment. I learned about this when I was living in Gurumayi's ashram. For about five months, I was directing hundreds of people through daily lineups at lunchtime. I began noticing that many people who spoke to me would offer an opinion about how I was feeling or looking that day. One person would say, "Oh, you look radiant today." But the very next person would say, "You look sad." Another would say, "You are so joyful." The next, "You are so serious," or "You are so wild." This continued for some time until I began to realize that each person was projecting his or her own state of mind onto me.

This upset me and I felt terribly lonely. It seemed as though no one truly saw me; I was only a backdrop for their state. I began to wonder if we truly connect as human beings at all. What is the point anyway? It seemed that people believed and saw only what they want to see. For a long time I experienced the emptiness and loss of what I had previously perceived as human relationships. I thought that all humans shared the same reality, but I came to realize that everyone lives in his or her own reality. I began to feel like a prostitute for other people's minds. Once I surrendered to my feeling of loss and sadness and came to accept it as the human condition, I began to see the love that is the true essence of every human being. Their opinions really don't matter much. Looking at another person was like looking at a perfect diamond with rhinestones surrounding it; I could put my attention on the rhinestones or the diamond. If I put my attention on the rhinestones, which signify falseness and separation, I would feel sad and lonely. If, however, my attention was on the diamond, the true Self, I would feel Love.

I even learned to laugh at what people said because I saw that they were actually talking about themselves. And I learned that what connects the form to the formless and us to one another is precious, pure, clear Love, which sees only perfection, even in the absurdity of projection.

Sometimes we feel so alone in our longing for another to reach out and touch us. The deepest pain we experience is that we are not seen in our divinity but only for our attributes and accomplishments. We all long to be seen as God sees us. When we acknowledge this longing, we can begin to be of service to those around us; we can look at them and see the God and the love in them, rather than merely focusing on the outer form. This is the true meaning of service.

As an antidote for projection, when you encounter each new person, silently say to yourself, "Thank you Lord for coming to me in this form." Capture projection itself before it finds a person or object to project upon. Look past the judgments that you may have about what you see and ask yourself, "Who sees?"

Meditation Keys – Projection

Recall a time in which you felt really happy. Remember how the people and surroundings felt to you and how you related to them.

Recall a time in which you felt unhappy. Remember how the people and surroundings felt to you while in this state.

Assuming that everything you see is you, spend a day experimenting with your projections with the awareness that whatever is reflected back to you is your own state of being.

Have the intention to know who you really are. Remember that you are not the projections that others place upon you.

PROJECTION

* Projection sees the world through its own perspective.
* Projection, if happy, sees others as wonderful. If sad or angry, it sees others as cold, harsh or distant.
* Projection judges everything according to its own feelings.
* Projection informs how we relate to others most of the time.
* Projection can tell us that we are beautiful one day and ugly the next based on how it feels.
* Projection is another trick of the negative power used to keep us busy making up realities so we never drop fully into the true Self.

They will pay

I am so angry
But I must hide it where nobody can find it –
in my heart
I will get back at them one day for all of their actions
But, in the meantime, I will sit here
Seething and waiting
But, I will smile when they come
So they won't know my plans and how much I want to
hurt them
This cruel feeling in me feels kind of good and
empowering
You say to let it go? No way!
Then, I will be made weak and vulnerable before them
And I will lose the power I need for my revenge
Oh, by the way, please close that door when you leave

Resentment

I once knew someone toward whom I carried a lot of resentment. When I spoke with him, I would seethe with anger as he seemed so uncaring and gruff toward me. I didn't tell him how I was feeling, so he kept treating me the same way. Over time, I became more and more resentful. I began to hate him; I even had thoughts of revenge for his mistreatment of me. One day, I finally had the courage to tell him how hurt I was by the way he'd been treating me over the years. After this conversation, he softened and became more vulnerable; he genuinely felt badly about how he had been acting toward me. After months of carrying this demon called resentment, and finally having a talk with my friend, I was surprised that the problem that had been tormenting me was resolved so easily and that my resentment so quickly melted away.

From this relationship, I learned that resentment is really self-created; we make others the target of our unexpressed anger. It doesn't always get worked out as easily as it did with my friend. Sometimes, when we express our long-denied feelings, the other party disavows their part in the interaction. This can leave us with even more resentment. We can see this in warring countries that have different cultures and values. Terrorism can erupt in such instances. Terrorism is a deep built up resentment that leads to what the terrorist mind believes to be justifiable revenge.

Resentment can arise from miscommunication, unmet desires, seeing the other as separate, and not respecting our differences but instead forcing our will on another. Such behaviour can create pain, suffering, resentment, and ultimately feelings of revenge. Resentment is another trick of the negative power to keep us separate from each other and from God. Resentment, like pride, can be found everywhere; it is so pervasive as to be invisible.

Resentment can be subtle or not so subtle. A friend told me that he stopped buying expensive cars because after parking on the street at night, the following morning, he'd frequently find nails driven into his tires or a long scratch along the side of the car. Such destruction seemed to have arisen from someone's resentment that another person might be more fortunate. A more common example occurs when we go into a store and the clerk is resentful at having to get up and serve us. We can feel resentful about situations that fail to meet our expectations or that arise from unexpressed anger. We can be resentful toward all manner of forces, including God, because we feel disappointed in our lot in life. Resentment differs from anger, which can come and go like a storm; resentment grabs anger and holds onto it, sometimes for a lifetime. It is the unspoken words of anger and disappointment that create the disease of resentment, which often festers in families after years of close proximity and unexpressed feelings. People cannot fail to disappoint us or make us angry, especially in those relationships toward which we have placed a lot of expectations. Resentment eats up the love that we have for others.

Resentment is a powerful door closer and a common feeling that arises when we believe that there is another out there, separate and apart from us, who can hurt us or keep something from us. Resentment doesn't let us see what is occurring in the moment; it colours everything with an attitude of separation, specialness, anger, fear, or pride. Since we are God and so are those whom we resent, we only hurt ourselves.

What then is the antidote to resentment? Forgiveness and compassion. We can capture resentment by first seeing our resentment toward others and by noticing our expectations of them. We must then put ourselves in their shoes and try to see their perspective. We need to have compassion for another's inability to feel compassion and for our own inability as well. And we need to forgive ourselves for all of the atrocities that stream through our own minds toward ourselves and others in every moment. After all, we share the same mind. We must truly work at understanding our oneness with all that is.

✤Meditation Keys – Resentment✤

🗝 *Think of someone toward whom you feel resentment. Feel your resentment toward this individual as fully as you can.*

🗝 *Now remove this person from your focus and let yourself be left with the raw feeling of resentment.*

🗝 *Feel the power of resentment, but instead of being caught in its web, offer it to God and ask that all be forgiven and returned to Love.*

RESENTMENT

* Resentment is anger gone wrong.
* Resentment colours everything with an attitude of separation.
* Resentment validates rebellious thoughts and blocks out love.
* Resentment holds onto the past and blackens the present.
* Resentment is based on "victim" consciousness often feeling hurt or hard-done-by.
* Resentment misuses power as it feels that it is justified in its actions. It uses control to get its own way.
* Resentment is revenge towards itself as well as others since it holds all beings out of the light of God.

Give it to me Now!

Hurry up – I have no time to waste!
I need it now!
Later will not do!
I've had enough of waiting
I want instant results
You speak of enlightenment?
So, give it to me!
Now! I want it now!
Don't laugh at me with that stupid, knowing grin
If I can't get it here, I'll go somewhere else
I haven't the time to be still to listen and experience
It can't be that great if it takes so much time
Life is too short!
I'd rather enjoy other pleasures
At least they are immediate
So I will close the door and leave here
And forget this momentary lapse
Returning to my world of the ticking clock.

Impatience

Understanding timing is one of the greatest keys to locking or unlocking the divine doorway. God's time, not our time, is what will truly serve us. However many of us are plagued by impatient thoughts, "I want it now. I'm sick of waiting." We've all felt this way. Unfortunately, impatience contracts us, and anything that is contracted pushes our desire further away from us. There is a saying: "Chase the world and the world runs away. Chase God and your desires come looking for you."

We all know impatience, that anxious, frightened, fearful feeling that we won't get what we need or want and that we must look to our surroundings to find it. In so doing, we lose the moment and we lose our lives. We are left angry, frustrated, depressed, victimized, abandoned, and empty.

Impatience is a trait that stems from the fear of not

being able to control our own life or the lives of others. We have an unrealistic expectation of ourselves that we must be on top of everything at all times. We must be the "doer" of all actions and we exert tremendous effort in order to make things happen. While putting forth effort is a good thing, the kind of effort that originates from impatience separates us from others and ultimately from God. This is because its motivation and focus are on the outer form of things.

Many years ago, I had a client who was brilliant intellectually and very successful. She ran a large company, had many employees working under her, but still felt afraid, anxious and impatient. She was very much a "doer," one who believes that she is alone and must do everything herself without the help or Grace of God. This belief extended to her relationships at work; she could not delegate assignments for she did not trust those who worked for her. Consequently, this cycle of fear, impatience and overwhelm consumed her. In a session one day, while we were discussing these issues, she realized that she had no trust or room for God in her life, although she would like to. So I had her do a little exercise every time that she was afraid or impatient. This exercise simply consisted of saying, "God please help me, I don't know what to do."

After a few weeks of doing this, she began to notice changes. She started to relax and felt less alone. Her intuition strengthened and she began to trust that things were going to be okay without her constant intervention. Her trust even extended to her relationships with employees. She began to delegate responsibilities, which empowered those around her. Everyone, including her, felt happier. My client's impatience became much less of an interference because every time it would arise, she would catch herself and repeat the refrain, "God please help me."

"I want it now!" Whenever we are around someone with this agenda, he or she seems harsh and uncaring. We are equally hard and harsh when we have no patience with others or with ourselves. Patience is the closest state to the divine Self. When we are patient we feel relaxed, kind, and flexible. We notice ourselves trusting the other person and trusting the unfolding of our lives. Patience has the quality of trust and peace, and of being in the moment. When we are patient, we enjoy every moment, as we are patient with life. This is not unlike a mother patiently watching as her child stumbles and falls learning to walk. Or the patience of a flower fully dependent on the rain, the sun, and the bees for its moment of glorious blossoming.Impatience is a closed door to the divine. Patience is actually a state of enlightenment.

What is the antidote to Impatience? Letting go and learning to trust that we are not alone and that God is waiting patiently for us to ask for help. It has been said, that for every step that we take towards God, He takes a thousand towards us. We must capture impatience before it runs into the future.

✤Meditation Keys✤

🗝 *Recall a recent moment in which you've been impatient with someone.*

🗝 *In that moment, what were you afraid would either happen or not happen?*

🗝 *Revisit that moment of impatience and reframe it. Imagine impatience arising but instead of acting out as before, take a deep breath, feel your fear, and ask God for help. Have the intention to trust that everything will work out perfectly, as needed for your soul's evolution.*

IMPATIENCE

* Impatience cuts us off from the joy in life.
* Impatience feels like anger to those who are around it.
* Impatience does not trust that life will unfold perfectly without its intervention. It has great expectations of others.
* Impatience carries great desire within it and strives to be in the next moment rather than this one.
* Impatience is based on fear.
* Impatience misses the beauty of connecting with others because it is in the future, whereas love exists in the present moment.

Rejecting The Moment

Resistance is the greatest enemy to inner peace. Not accepting what life offers in the moment causes us so much pain. When we resist what is, we feel such guilt and anxiety because we think we should be somewhere else experiencing something different. We think that who we are is not okay. We believe that we'll relax and be happy "if only..." But following the "if only's" never allows our true joy to be experienced in the present situation or moment. Consequently, we miss what is right in front of us.

Resistance arises when we are looking for what we can get from this world. How can we enhance our good position? How can we get others to see us, acknowledge us, love us? How can we get something from them? Like animals stalking our prey or protecting and defending our territory, we wait for the new and improved future that never comes.

Our world is a fear-based reality, which comes from not

knowing the true purpose for taking on a human form. We are not here "to get stuff." We are here to pierce the wall of appearances and enter into the heart of life, where our only purpose is to experience God in each moment and in each person we encounter. This is not possible as long as we are resisting our life or rejecting what IS in this moment.

When we are in resistance, love becomes conditional because we are always grasping or fighting in some way. Love becomes bargaining, based on "If you do this for me, I'll do that for you." If favors aren't returned, resentment builds because we didn't get our "piece of the action." When we don't resist what is presented in the moment, including unpleasant circumstances, we enter into our hearts, which connects us to the Love inherent in all things. It takes courage to be with life as it is now. We must practice appreciation and gratitude for the lessons life offers. This is what it means to enter into life.

When we break through the wall of resistance, usually by getting tired of it, we are able to experience appreciation for each moment. What may have appeared to be devastating comes into true perspective when we relax and let it be. We get to watch the same situation go from extreme contraction to expansion. The outside may not necessarily change but our inner experience does, and that is where happiness comes from.

Nothing exists except our own Self. When we finally realize there is no way out of the maze, we can truly find an attitude of peace and acceptance in our lives. Until we tire ourselves out, the journey to surrender often involves a lot of pain, anger, and fighting arising from our resistance. Finally, we give up. This giving up is not a weakness or in anyway negative, but is instead a sur-rendering or letting go of expectations, which always end in disappointment and suffering anyway. Embracing life as it unfolds in each moment strengthens our trust in God. Then, we can stop running away from fear and we can die into this moment.

The antidote for resistance is gratitude for every moment in life. Capture the energy of resistance before it erases the precious moments of your life.

✤Meditation Keys – Rejecting the Moment✤

☛ *Contemplate a situation in your life that you really don't like.*

☛ *Let yourself feel the fight and frustration of wanting this situation to be different. Let yourself accept this resistance without fighting it.*

☛ *Write down all the ways that you want the situation to be different.*

☛ *Now think of one thing in your life that you are grateful for.*

☛ *Sit quietly in the peace that this gratitude brings.*

REJECTING THE MOMENT

* Resistance is non-acceptance of what is.
* Resistance's favorite words are "if only."
* Resistance fears arriving in the moment because it means death to separation.
* Resistance will not be happy until all of its desires are met.
* Resistance avoids the open spaces between thoughts out of fear of falling through and vanishing.

Yesterday and Tomorrow

Oh the past was so much greater than now
I was younger, smarter, stronger, sexier, richer
I could do almost anything
I could almost fly
Now, life seems boring and dull
And aging is really not much fun
Oh, but maybe the future holds promise
Maybe if I just won the lottery I'd be happy
I'd live on a tropical island and bask in the sun
I'd build a house where I could roam and dance
And maybe even you would come
Yes, that's it!
Lets think of tomorrow
It's so much more fun
Live in the moment now, you say?
What?
And pierce my fantasies of tomorrow?
No, I say – go away
It hurts too much to be here now
I must stay distracted so come with me
I will show you how to avoid that open door
That will swallow you and dissolve you
And leave nothing but an eternal now
Wait, you're opening that door, please keep it closed!

Dwelling On The Past

R ecently, I looked at an old photo of myself in which I looked radiant and hopeful, and then looked in the mirror only to see someone wrinkled and tired. I realized just how sad I felt about my lost youth. I also realized how short our lives are and how much time we spend distracted in the past wishing for the joys of days gone by. I am different now and that person in the picture is gone forever; all I really have is this moment. The past is irretrievable – trying to reclaim it is like grasping at thin air. The past was not solid or real in any case; it was merely a succession of events.

When we live in the past, we are not living life now. It seems so simple and obvious, but most of us fail to realize that in denying this moment in favor of some past moment, we are denying and judging our very existence. If we are unhappy with our present life, we may escape to a more desirable era or experience in the past. There is a definite sense of loss for what once was as we compare our present life with how things used to be. Invariably, the present falls far short. This may be why, like the aging movie star played by Gloria Swanson in *Sunset Boulevard*, some famous people become recluses or commit suicide when they age and lose their looks or persona.

It truly is a sad state of affairs when we live in our minds, trying to grasp the pictures as they go by. It only amplifies the emptiness we feel underlying every experience. The benefit of revisiting the past is the opportunity to witness the impermanence of the illusion in which we live. Recognizing that we can no longer hold onto the past can bring us to an understanding of our true and eternal nature. We then have the wisdom to see that the past is history and can never be retrieved.

So what is the antidote to living in the past? Thanking each and every moment for the gift that it is giving to us. Then everything that we eat becomes nectar and everything that we see becomes a gift that we will never see again in this way. Everything that we feel becomes an opportunity to feel the love of God; everything that we hear – the ocean, voices, silence – becomes music. And every word that we speak can proclaim our gratitude for the moment and sing the praises of the Divine.

✣Meditation Keys – Dwelling on the Past✣

🔑 *Sit for 10 minutes and imagine a shower of light washing through your whole being, cleansing you of the heaviness of clinging to the past.*

🔑 *Rest in the freedom and weightlessness of just being in this moment.*

DWELLING ON THE PAST

* The past always looks better than the present.
* The past is filled with fantasies of a life that seemed more fulfilling.
* The past places a heavy burden on our shoulders, carrying it forward into the future.
* Living in the past can lead to great grief because of the inevitable loss of time and opportunity.
* The past creates a longing for itself which turns into sadness instead of a longing for the true Self which turns into joy.

Fixating On The Future

We are always planning for the future in one way or another. We can observe this in others when we walk down the street. Trying to meet their gaze, we see that many of them have gone somewhere else, usually into the next moment. They aren't home. We all live like this unless we are able to deeply relax. We think about what food we'll eat, whom we'll meet, or when we will be finished with this meeting or bank line-up, or when we will get out of this traffic jam. We spend our time thinking about what the weekend will bring and how much happier we'll be. It never stops. We travel to a future time, which dissolves as soon as we get there, necessitating that a new future be created. In doing this, we vacate the moment that we're in. The desire to not be here in this moment is insatiable; it is another trick of the negative power to keep us separate from God. Resisting the moment for a future desire robs us of the miracles and ecstasies that are waiting to be discovered here and now.

If we do show up for life for a few minutes, we may only stay long enough until our next daydream preoccupies our minds.

So what is the antidote for fixating on the future? It is the same as for the past. Every time that we run away into some future time, we stop, back up, and find the richness in this moment. We thank each and every moment for the gift that it is giving us.

✤Meditation Keys – Fixating on the Future✤

🗝 *Sit for 10 minutes and imagine a shower of light washing through your whole being cleansing you of the anxiety of trying to get to a nonexistent future.*

🗝 *Rest in the stillness and emptiness that remains.*

FIXATING ON THE FUTURE

* The future always looks better than the present.
* The future is filled with fantasies of a life that will soon arrive and remove all of our problems.
* The future always has one foot out the door for fear that it might miss something.
* The future is like a drug; it is unquenchable.
* The future's longing is for change in the outer world rather than living in the now.

Making Dragons from Nothing

I'm so worried that it won't work out the way I've
planned
I won't be on time
They won't like me
My presentation will fail
Oh, I am so worried
I know I won't sleep tonight
I have a million reasons for which to worry
You say that I make big dragons out
of the smallest things
But they are real and will overtake and chew me up
I'm tight and I'm scared, and I'm sure that the worst
will happen
How can I get free from this?
"Who do you think you are?" – you're asking me
Well don't you know?
I'm that woman on television…
I've had lots of recognition
I have an image to live up to
Who wouldn't worry?
What if I fail?
Then I'll become an amorphous being
Without a face
Please close and lock that door as you leave, I'm afraid
someone may rob me.

Worry

Don't worry, whatever is supposed to come always comes, it never fails. Face everything contentedly while absorbing your mind in the Lord.

                                                    Lalleshwari

"Don't worry, be happy" is a phrase that many of us have heard, but living it is easier said than done. Worry is based on a lack of trust. Have you ever tried to calm someone who is worrying? It is very difficult because worry is like an addiction that grips the heart and mind of the worrier; it has a life of its own. At the root of worry is the fear of death. Worry is another weapon of the negative power that grabs the mind and separates us from God.

I have a friend named Paddy, who used to say, "I have long felt that our body is really just a big plastic bag of blood. The object of the exercise is to get through life without springing a leak and having the fluids escape."

This is a graphic depiction of worry. At the level of the body, how can we not worry? However, if we experience ourselves as "deathless" and one with God, then worry can be no more.

What is the antidote for worry? When we begin to worry, recognize it as a nudge to return to our hearts deep wisdom that knows only trust. Know that everything comes from God to take us back home, a home of faith and trust. Capture worry before it grabs hold of the next problem.

✦Meditation Keys✦

⚷ *Choose a situation that you find worrisome. Imagine yourself as a cartoon character who is out of control with worry about it.*

⚷ *As that character, let yourself have fun with your worry, as though it has nothing to do with you personally.*

⚷ *As you play with worry, allow some distance to take place between you and the situation. If there is something that you can do to alleviate that situation then do it.*

⚷ *If, however, the situation is completely out of your control, then practice offering the source of worry, your involvement, and any outcome over to God. Know that God already understands your every need.*

WORRY

* Worry feels that if it "worries," only then will things be under control.
* Worry is based on a belief in lack, separation, and fear.
* Worry is exhausting.
* Worry usually creates horrible scenarios, much worse than what may realistically happen.
* Worry lives totally in the future basing its fear on the past.
* Worry has no trust or faith.

The Green-Eyed Monster

How come they can have it and I can't?
I'm just as smart, just as good looking, just as worthy
I hate them!
You're telling me that a green-eyed monster is choking
my life
But I feel like a black panther that wants to swat away
all that they have
You say that I will be more content when I can
appreciate another's good fortune?
They have no right to be happy!
I want them to fail - to suffer!
To know what I've been through
Let them feel as lowly and wretched as I do
Then they'd know what it is to be the loser
I want to string them up so the whole world can laugh
at their downfall
Only then will I feel the war has been won
This is all I have to say now, so please close the door
behind you

Jealousy

She came to Envy's house, a black abode, ill-kept, stained with dark gore, a hidden home in a deep valley, where no sunshine comes, where no wind blows, gloomy and full of cold...

Ovid

Envy or jealousy is appreciation gone wrong. When we look at another's great qualities, we feel jealousy because we believe that he or she is separate and better than us. So we covet their good qualities and want them for ourselves. What we fail to recognize is that God has created many different people with many different talents for many different purposes, which are designed to help us experience the unique lessons that we are here on this earth to learn. In the *Bhagavad Gita*, Lord Krishna said that it is better for one to do his own dharma, one's true purpose, no matter how humbly or poorly, than to do another's dharma, however impressively or well.

Many of the saints say that our lives are already laid out for us, that our life is destined and what we need to do is to graciously accept our purpose in life. The difficulty is that we don't have the support for that in this world; certain careers are looked upon more favorably than others and are given recognition by way of fame and fortune. Children are often not encouraged to follow their true dharma, which is their Divine calling. The media gives children the subliminal and often overt suggestion that it is better to go after fame and fortune. I know many great artists who were sensitive children demeaned for not fitting in. Not having chosen mainstream careers as adults, they have spent much of their lives being jealous of others who followed a more conventional path with more money and worldly success.

Our world is quite different from how it appears. There is a covering that veils our eyes, causing us to see ourselves as separate and to jealously obsess about one another. In so doing, we lose our connection with God's Love. Jealousy stifles Love and cuts off life at its root. How different it would be if we were taught that jealousy is actually an appreciation of someone and their good qualities or talents, and that all such gifts come from God. Then we could watch the great dance in which we are all participating, awestruck at the greatness that we see in others and in ourselves, for we too have God-given gifts.

A friend was telling me about a talk that Gurumayi had once given about jealousy and envy. He told me that many people wanted to sit close to her in the meditation hall. Although the hall could comfortably hold hundreds of people, jealousies were arising because many people wanted to be chosen to sit in front near Gurumayi. They were envious of those who were seated there. Noticing this, Gurumayi said that if anyone was feeling jealousy toward another, to know that it is really "you" that you are looking at, not another person. If someone else is experiencing good fortune in their lives, know that you are also experiencing good fortune in your life.

If we were to come from the perspective of wholeness, we'd be truly happy for each other as we'd know that all talents and gifts we see in others are God-given. We would be more able to cultivate our own greatness, not from ego, pride or competitiveness, but from gratitude and appreciation. There would be no need for jealousy or envy. In the meantime, when we are experiencing these feelings, we can use them as an opportunity to practice appreciation.

The antidote to jealousy is gratitude for the gifts that God has given to us. The art is to capture jealousy before it finds an object or person to covet.

✤Meditation Keys – Jealousy✤

🗝 *Choose a person toward whom you feel jealous.*

🗝 *Let the power of the jealousy build inside you.*

🗝 *Ask yourself what this person has that you want.*

🗝 *Imagine that he or she is just a part of you being reflected back. If you like that part so much, know that it is alive and well in your own life.*

🗝 *Contemplate jealousy as another form of God designed to take you to the understanding, "I am all that exists."*

JEALOUSY

* Jealousy is based on unworthiness, incomplete-ness, and a belief that there is something outside of us to "get."
* Jealousy is a form of greed.
* Jealousy obsesses over the smallest things and wishes misfortune on the perceived competitor.
* Jealousy is deeply self-absorbed and cares only for its own end.
* Jealousy has created wars because of the belief that there is an "us" and a "them."
* Jealousy lives in great separation and duality, not knowing that all that exists is the one Self.
* Jealousy is appreciation gone wrong.

Oh How Imperfect am I

Oh…look at me
I am so shameful
A disgrace to be alive
Don't come too close to me
You will see all my terrible imperfections
I'm a failure
I'm weak
I'm afraid
I'm not lovable
My pores sweat poison
You are so lucky
You are so much better than I -
So much wiser
So much more attractive
You know how to be a somebody
While I, on the other hand, hate what I am
And writhe and squeeze inside this body
As if a hundred boa constrictors lived there
"Come out and shine your light," you say
No, I must hide myself in a corner
Away from the light
So that my shame can merge into the darkness
Close that door please, its way too bright in here

Unworthiness

Brooding over our faults and unworthiness is just one way to resign, to close the book to new experience in all its complexity. We resign, we steadfastly refuse to forgive the sources of these internalized insinuations and insults; we fold our arms and we make ourselves miserable.

Richard Mann

Feelings of unworthiness have been a major challenge in my life. As a child, I was the older sister of two brothers who incessantly teased me about my appearance. When I was ten or eleven, my nose was too long as the rest of me hadn't yet caught up and I felt like the ugliest thing in the world. Compounding this, I was the youngest in my class because I had skipped a couple of grades, and since I hadn't yet developed breasts, the other kids used to punch me in the chest for being flat-chested. Hoping to feel more worthy, I sent away for breast exercisers, which of course didn't work. I felt criticized a lot as a child, and I also felt ignored by my father. Working hard to overcome my self-hatred, I became a perfectionist. As an adolescent, I would examine every little pimple on my face in an attempt to improve. Once I matured, I became a model, which put me in another league of dancing with unworthiness and perfectionism. The first time my picture was on a magazine cover, I ran home so fast, I could have won a marathon race, just to show my dad. I said, "Dad, look at me!" But the underlying feeling was, "Am I worthy yet?" Even though I have experienced success in my life at times, this deep unworthiness has always lurked just beneath the surface. Then, in those times when my external life was not meeting my standards, I would consider giving up life entirely.

Reflecting on my early life, the pain of unworthiness became so great, that it forced me to look for, and find, the doorway to my true worth, where there is no judgment or lack of Love. From God's perspective, every breath is Divine and precious. My earlier life was perfectly designed so that I would seek truth and love only to find it deep within the one I most hated – myself. The 14th century Christian mystic Meister Eckhart wrote, "God expects but one thing of you, and that is that you should come out of yourself in so far as you are a created being, and let God be God in you." [19]

The only way out of the maze of self-hatred and unworthiness is to become free of the identification with the body, thoughts, emotions, or personality. Also, in order to love, we must understand the trap of unworthiness that separates us from the Self and from others. Unworthiness may draw into our current lives a similar abusiveness that we may have encountered in childhood. This cycle can replay itself repeatedly, which can lead to the mistaken belief that we somehow deserve this abuse. Some people may try to make up for their "deficiency" by abusing others themselves.

According to Gurumayi, "The feeling of unworthiness creates disrespect if we do not feel the greatness or divinity in ourselves, if we do not experience the truth within, how can we recognize the greatness and the truth in others?" [20] Since love and acceptance of all that we are is the key to opening the door, we must give up old belief systems that tell us that the way we are is not enough. We must recognize that unworthiness is a complete lie that is based upon old conditioned ways of thinking. If we grab hold of these thoughts as they pass by, we create a hellish reality. The belief that we are unworthy implies that we do not know *who we really are*. When we know *who we really are*, unworthiness disappears. We must ask ourselves "Who is it that feels unworthy?"

The antidote to unworthiness is humility before God. We must remember that everything that we are has been perfectly created by God for the perfect reason. Capture the unworthiness before it grabs hold of any negative self-talk.

✤Meditation Keys – Unworthiness ✤

☛ *The next time you feel unworthy, stop, and notice the thoughts that are associated with this feeling of unworthiness.*

☛ *Notice what these thoughts are saying about you.*

☛ *Observe yourself listening to the thoughts. As if listening to an old worn-out tape, see yourself choosing not to believe this tape anymore, no matter how convincing it may sound.*

☛ *Imagine yourself physically throwing the tape away with the understanding that it has nothing to do with you.*

☛ *Begin to identify yourself with The One Who is Watching these thoughts. Become the Witness so that the energy of unworthiness can serve as a reminder of your true worth.*

Affirmations

☛ *Day One. Affirm "I am enough, I am enough" for a full day.*

☛ *Day Two. Affirm "I Am, I Am" for a full day.*

☛ *Day Three. Affirm "I am enough" for a number of minutes and then "I Am." Then listen to the silence in the moment that goes beyond any words. Let yourself rest where true worth resides.*

UNWORTHINESS

* Unworthiness has a very strong ego identity as a victim and a failure.
* Unworthiness is humility gone wrong.
* Unworthiness is experienced as powerlessness and fear and can lead to rebelliousness and rage.
* Unworthiness draws abusive situations to itself.
* Unworthiness is overcompensated for by perfectionism and needing to prove its worth. Its alter ego is "I am better than you."
* Unworthiness arises from having received a lot of criticism as a child.
* Unworthiness doesn't feel deserving of the light of God.

Give me more of everything!

Fill me, fill me, fill me
Don't stop until I can't take anymore
Let me eat
Let me listen
Let me speak
Let me smell
Let me drink
Now, give me more
I need more
If I don't have these things, I feel empty
I can't stand that feeling, so make the music louder
Make the cake sweeter
Make the liquor stronger
Make the sex longer
You want me to leave gaps for that
open space of Divinity?
It's too painful
It's too quiet
It's too boring
You're telling me all of my senses will be filled with
nectar if I stop and become silent?
I'm too afraid to stop because I know the grief I've felt
when I could not fill my desires
And please close that door as you leave so I can sleep
as this visit has made me very tired

Overindulgence

We have been given eyes to see, ears to hear, mouths to taste, a nose to smell and touch to feel. If respected, these senses can bring us to ecstasy. Our problems begin when we overindulge them with too much caffeine, food, sex, alcohol, cigarettes, drugs, loud noise, TV, computers, or other distractions that keep us from the infinite bliss and joy of our inner life. Our senses are not unlike delicate flowers that are meant to be treated with tenderness and love, yet we often abuse and therefore underutilize them. God has given us these senses for enjoyment and for experiencing the Truth.

Overindulgence is greed of the senses. We can enjoy ourselves in a balanced manner, but when we tip the scale toward greed, we suffer. There are times when a glass of wine is enjoyable, but on a day when we have had trouble with our employer, or a fight with our spouse, that one enjoyable glass can become two, three or even four... By then the senses are numbed and out of touch with *who we really are*. This is another way that the negative power tempts us away from our God self, by creating cravings for alcohol, drugs, sex, food, or whatever else we are drawn to rather than facing life in that moment. Many of us have numbed ourselves out in order to cope with life and our daily stresses. Loud music, toxic smells, construction noises, constant visual stimulation, stress, pressure, and traffic of both cars and people, often lead to prescription drug use or other potentially addictive measures to enable us to cope.

Through the senses, we can easily slip through the magic doorway to the Divine Self. But we cannot enter the door while carrying the baggage of overindulgence. One of the reasons people pursuing a spiritual life initially change their diet and lifestyle, is to develop greater sensitivity and to open themselves to the subtle inner energies. As long as the senses are over-taxed, the door remains closed. In the process, the great potential of our beautiful Divine senses is suppressed. We need time and space to feel and taste our own inner love. After refining our senses, our taste buds become so alive that we can eat a mere seed and experience bliss. Our ears are able to hear the celestial music that comes from within. Our eyes can see profound beauty in a mere leaf or a pebble. Our sense of touch can become so heightened, that when we are with our intimate partners, we can enter into a heavenly state.

Looking to the outer form to fill the soul's hunger will never work; the soul can only be filled with the inner nectar. We have a deep well inside, for which we have endlessly searched in our outer worlds. This well fulfills every one of our needs. Initially, our senses may need to be protected from the constant barrage of outer stimuli and redirected to the subtle inner kingdom. Through meditation, we can begin to return to ourselves and use our senses to drink from this well. Overindulgence will naturally fall away, without any need for therapy or other more invasive approaches. The senses will become so divinely alive that they will indicate to us their appropriate limitations, without struggle.

What is the antidote to overindulgence? Gratitude for what we already have. Through meditation, we can let our cravings take us to a world of bliss within. By asking what we are truly craving, we can capture overindulgence before we give into it.

✢Meditation Keys – Overindulgence ✢

☞ *Spend some time becoming quiet and still. Then, like a scientist, explore the gift of the senses. Focus all of your attention inside and observe what happens.*

☞ *Allow yourself to look, listen, taste, and breathe from the well of nourishment that exists within the silence.*

☞ *If your senses reach to something external, return to this inner well of silence and breathe in Love.*

☞ *Let Love be the salve for all of your empty senses that are tired of all of this outward seeking.*

OVERINDULGENCE

* Overindulgence is the suppression of the God Self. It knows that it is actually craving the divine nectar of God.
* Overindulgence's "enjoyment" turns into poison in the end.
* Overindulgence stuffs its grief and pain with all manner of worldly delights.
* Overindulgence has the maturity of an unsupervised two-year-old in a candy store.
* Overindulgence carries a lot of rage and fear.

I want to devour you

I want to devour you
Merge with you
You're asking me about love?
Don't show me your humanness or your weakness or
talk about love
It will shatter my fantasy of you
It will disappoint me and I will have to come tumbling
down
To the denseness and frailty of this human form
I don't want any of this, it will turn me off
I want to escape into my fantasy
I want to design you to be my perfect doll
With no imperfections
Not too much vulnerability please
I don't need to know who you are
Unless some of this might serve to spark my desire
So please – hide yourself and show me only what I
want to see
So let's close the door
So we can have that one moment of ecstasy

Luſt

ust is one of our greatest temptations. I once read that many people reincarnate in order to fulfill lust. We feel pulled by lust because, at the moment of orgasm, we experience the ecstasy of God. But lust demands that we seek gratification through others' bodies. Not only is dealing with their attendant feelings a lot of work, but unconscious lust is a misuse of others.

For many years, sex was a major focus in my life. People would laugh and say that it was because I am a Scorpio. Whatever the reason, my entire reality revolved around experiencing and fulfilling this drive. But after I experienced *who I really am*, I developed a different orientation towards sex. The sexual energy that I experienced during my enlightenment experience was so strong that my previous understanding of lust and sex changed completely; I discovered that sexual energy and God are one and the same. At first I was overcome by its intensity but over time, as I learned to work with it, I saw that it was the energy of oneness. The God energy I was feeling could just as easily emerge from communion with a tree as with a person. With every chakra experiencing complete orgasm, the feeling in the body would be the same. When we are ready to merge with God, the energy that habitually goes outward after the external form, is focused instead on the soul. The resulting fusion of souls lifts us into realms of unspeakable bliss that a moment of mere physical orgasm could never satisfy. Since that time, the longing that I had previously projected onto men, was rerouted to the inherent love and bliss that comes from within. Nothing in the external world can satisfy our hunger to make love with The Creator.

Lust, greed, anger, pride are all reminders to focus our attention on God by whom all of our desires will be continually fulfilled. Lust toward our partner can be healthy when he or she is held in a place of respect. There is nothing wrong with lust if we know its nature and are not controlled by it. We can observe it passing through the mind without attaching to it or engaging it. Lust only separates us from others when we misuse it by objectifying and disrespecting them. An all-too-common example is the guru, priest, or teacher who preaches celibacy only to be overtaken by lust and indulge in inappropriate behaviour with young disciples, students, or acolytes. But seeing God in the other, and making love to the God in him or her with absolute respect for *who he or she really is*, is the ultimate experience of love and worship in the human form.

Although everything has a higher purpose and we can

become stronger from our experiences, there comes a time when we need to evolve. In other words, we need to learn to take greater responsibility for our sexual energy. Our sexual energy is Divine at essence, and when it moves through the human system at its highest vibration, it can merge us with Truth. When we merge with God, we experience a sexual fulfillment far greater than anything we have ever known. The Oneness that we have sought in others' bodies lives inside us and makes love to us every moment of the day. Once we've experienced Divine love, there is no going back.

The antidote for lust is remembering that all that we are seeking from another already exists within us a hundred fold. The lesson is to capture lust before it is projected outward onto another and to direct the mind to experience the blessings within.

✤Meditation Keys – Lust✤

Recall a moment when you have lusted after someone.

Feel the sensations in your body. Notice your thoughts.

Take away the object of your lust and allow yourself to feel the raw energy moving through you. Take away the label "lust," and observe this sensation and how it has a life of its own.

Notice that once you have removed the label and the person toward whom you had been lusting, you experience the raw energy of the God Self, making love to your body. Bask in this feeling and open up to this energy. Know it to be your own light.

Repeat this practice the next time you find yourself lusting after someone.

LUST

* Lust is a collection of mental pictures that get projected onto another human being. Once the real person is revealed, lust tends to dissipate.
* Lust wants only to fulfill its own needs and will lie and manipulate to get what it wants.
* Lust is one of the most powerful energies in the universe.
* Lust has destroyed gurus, great leaders, and politicians.
* Lust is not love.
* Lust can turn into obsession and addiction.

It can't be true

I know I've touched the light and felt completely loved
But right now, everything seems so ordinary and mundane
I feel my earlier experience must have been some kind of
fantasy
After all, who was that person who was so happy and
free?
What, you're telling me that that's who I really am?
But nobody supports my experience, so it can't be true
A million people can't be wrong
If someone comes along to confirm me, then maybe I'll
reconsider
But, in the meantime, I will turn my face away from this
light
And slot back into what I'm used to
So please close that door so I can get back to sleep

Doubt

We have become so falsely "sophisticated" and neurotic that we take doubt itself for truth, and the doubt that is nothing more than the ego's desperate attempt to defend itself from wisdom is deified as the goal and fruit of true knowledge.

Sogyal Rinpoche

Doubt is another one of those dark veils that prevents us from seeing the light of God. Have you ever experienced a moment in which you knew something to be true and from your heart? But then you meet someone and tell him or her your experience, and by the time he or she has left, you have lost your sense of conviction. The voice of the soul is a quiet voice, and it gently seeps into our consciousness with pearls of wisdom when we least expect it. Doubt squashes this voice of the soul because it has more power. This is because the majority of people believe that what you see is what you get and the deeper soul-wisdom is seen as questionable. This is why we have a hard time trusting ourselves.

Self-doubt is a great demon and it plagues us constantly. If we are confused and we disregard our inner Self or soul, we will separate ourselves from God, and wonder if our previous experiences have any validity at all. Half the time, we will doubt that God even exists. This is why we fall into the "doer" or strong self-will that carries no hope for help other than that provided by our personality self. But doubt does have a purpose. As with pride, greed, lust and anger, we can focus it toward the Truth. Then, instead of doubting the soul's small voice, we can use our doubt to question our ego attachment to thinking that we know the answers. We can challenge our unconscious drive for linear answers to explain reality; we can unveil our fear that what we are looking for is not in our control. We can do as a Hindu master once said and "Turn the dogs of doubt on doubt itself, to unmask cynicism and to uncover what fear, despair, hopelessness and tired conditioning it springs from. Then doubt would no longer be an obstacle but a door to realization, and whenever doubt appeared in the mind, a seeker would welcome it as a means of going deeper into the truth." [21]

The antidote to doubt, is to doubt your doubting. As Ramana Maharshi said, "When the doubter ceases, doubt will cease." It is only when we don't know who we really are that doubting can exist. When we know our authentic Self, there is no room for doubting.

✦Meditation Keys – Doubt✦

Recall a time when you have felt doubt.

Seeing it as the separate entity that it is, notice everything that doubt tells you about yourself.

Listen to the doubt as though as if it were a stranger, and then thank it.

Now listen to your heart's gentle prompting and follow that.

DOUBT

* Doubt is a shadow designed to darken any truth that one has experienced.
* Doubt makes us believe that the world of form is much more powerful than the world of the inner Self, because it is visible to the eye.
* Doubt is like the devil that wants us to live in the small and limited personality self rather than from our greatness.
* Doubt squeezes the joy, love, conviction, and faith from our hearts leaving us paralyzed and floundering.

I am such a wretch

I am so impure
I did a terrible thing
I know I shouldn't have done it, but I did
I should have done it another way
But I didn't
I don't deserve the love of God
So I will make sure none of it enters into my heart
How could I, wretched as I am, receive love?
You're telling me that God is all compassionate and
will forgive me?
I can't believe that...
No, I must reject it
For as many lives as I may live until I have paid for my
sins
So I must continue on my way and keep away from the
light and love
Oh, so you're saying that God's pure love will free me?
No, I did the action so I really must suffer for it
Thank you though; maybe we'll meet again someday.
Look I'm really sorry about being so messed up
So I'll just close the door for now
I hope you don't mind

Guilt

I was brought up Catholic and was taught from an early age that I was born a sinner and was inherently bad. I was also taught to be afraid of the nuns who beat my mother every day when she was attending school. Nuns were my Sunday school teachers and I remember being failed on an exam because I said that I didn't believe God judged humans as harshly as they claimed. Somewhere in my heart, I knew that I was loved deeply.

Catholicism has evolved since my childhood, but this example demonstrates the conditioning that has gone on for centuries, not only for Catholics but for believers from many other religions as well. It would seem that the negative power uses control and guilt to stomp out our inherent knowing that we are absolutely loved for *who we really are*. Organized religions may fear that allowing individuals to be free and uncontrollable in their direct connection with God would potentially negate their existence and power.

Guilt is a double-edged sword. On one side, we believe, "I did something I shouldn't have." And on the other side, we believe "I didn't do something that I should have." How many times in just one day do we run across this tendency in small ways, whether it be at work, with friends, or with family? Guilt gets into our system and tortures us. Guilt keeps us in duality – bad versus good, right versus wrong... As a consequence, we are out of connection with God who represents love, compassion and forgiveness.

As a little child writing the exam administered by the nuns, I knew that God loved me exactly as I was with all of my imperfections and that the God that they were speaking about was not real. Even though I have been plagued with guilt my whole life because of my conditioning, I have had the great good fortune to experience myself as one with God, where no right or wrong, good or bad exist. At the root of guilt is the belief that we have either performed an act that was bad or we haven't performed an act that we should have. To extend this logic, all of this doing or not doing is our responsibility. We will suffer for anything that we think that we have done wrong, which means that the issue is not so much with the action as with the belief that we are the doers of action. Advaita Master Ramesh Balsekar teaches that our body is "a body-mind organism" that is predestined and has been programmed to have certain experiences in this life. He says that we are ultimately not the doers of actions; our thoughts come from consciousness and are really not ours as we might believe. According to Ramesh Balsekar,

"If you seek peace in this life, then the only

thing to understand is that you are not the doer and that you're truly not responsible for anything that you do. But that doesn't mean that you have to be irresponsible. Because the answer ultimately is do whatever you like according to any standards of morality and responsibility you have. The standards of morality and responsibility are part of the programming, and you cannot act other than your programming." [22]

Since guilt has been such a challenge in my life, Ramesh Balsekar's teaching has returned me to a state of profound peace. The belief that God is doing the actions keeps me more connected to Love and I can then naturally choose actions that are uplifting and noble.

A friend once asked me, "If we have truly wronged someone, how do we make the distinction between the responsibility, or remorse, that we would feel for that action and ego-based guilt, or identification with being the doer of the action?" The response depends on the level from which we approach it. Remorse is an intuitive prompting that arises when we know that we have hurt someone; it is a good thing because it keeps us aware of how we are treating one other and shows us where we may need to be more caring in the future. One person's nature/programming may be to not harm another. Remorse or conscience therefore arises when he or she has mistreated another so that the appropriate action may be taken to rectify the situation. Then there are others who are not conscious of their actions because their programming/nature does not experience remorse. This thinking helps us to better understand the remorseless, criminal mind that is not adverse to causing harm or injury to others. The ultimate surrendering to God is the absolute knowing that God does all actions and there are no mistakes.

We must remember the mystery of this creation – even our own actions may come about in ways that surprise us. If we are able to look at our actions from a more expanded perspective, we realize that there is something much larger than our mind's limited ideas of good and bad taking place. I heard it once said that if you want to make God laugh, tell Him your plans.

From studying many scriptures and teachings, and from asking many masters about destiny and free will, what I've come to understand is that if we believe that we are the doer, then we will suffer the consequences and will feel guilt. On the other hand, if we truly know in our heart that God does all actions, and if we fully surrender to this understanding while graciously accepting life as it unfolds, then we do not need to suffer guilt. As we practise remembering who does everything, we can forgive ourselves and others; we will understand that God's plans may not always match our plans or our ideas about the "right" way of doing something.

Many people become reactive when they hear about the concept of nondoing. I've watched people become extremely angry as they insist that all of their actions are their own and that they have the power to change anything that they want with their thoughts. But where do these thoughts and actions come from? One day, I was sitting in a meditation group and when I opened my eyes, I saw the facilitator walk by me. I was shocked and thought, "How does he walk?" Then he spoke and again I was in awe and thought, "How does he talk?" I could not believe what I was witnessing. I realized that we do not perform a single action alone from our own strength. On our own, we do nothing. I could see the power of God moving him around. The facilitator was just a puppet and he was not in control of anything that he was doing. It is difficult to describe this experience in words but in that moment I knew, beyond a shadow of a doubt, what was meant by the Biblical saying, "There but for the grace of God go I."

If we could adopt this understanding, that it is only by God's grace that anything happens, there would be great peace and no room for guilt or pride, for what is there to be proud of, if we are not the doers of action? Nor would there be any need for fear or worry because we would know that our life and everything in it continually comes from God. Surrender would replace the ego sense of "I did it."

The antidote to guilt is surrendering our small and limited wills to God's Divine plan. Our sense of doing is a major door closer to knowing the truth of who we really are. If we can capture guilt as soon as we identify it, it can serve as a reminder to once again surrender our selves, our actions, and the fruits of our actions to God.

✤Meditation Keys – Guilt✤

⟐━━┳ *Think of a time when you've felt guilty.*

⟐━━┳ *Notice the belief that you were the one who performed the action that gave rise to guilt.*

⟐━━┳ *Imagine sitting before your God Self, confessing all that you believe that you did or didn't do, and offering it back to God. Feel your burden drop away as the power of Love forgives all.*

⟐━━┳ *Now look back on that situation in which you felt guilty and ask yourself, "Who does anything?"*

GUILT

* Guilt believes it is the doer of all action, which places it in duality, making it separate from God.

* Guilt is one of the greatest door closers as it is the root of karma itself – an eye for an eye, a tooth for a tooth.

* Guilt has great conviction about its impurity and wants to suffer either consciously or unconsciously to make up for it.

* Guilt does not want to go near the light of forgiveness because its nature is all-encompassing.

* Guilt dissolves when we truly understand that not one breath is taken without the grace of God.

Stepping Out of the Circle

I n working with the Door Closers, I had the opportunity to witness the great mystery of being in
God's playground and seeing how God uses everything including contradiction and duality to create the
uniqueness of our many experiences. From this I saw
how everything in life is conceptual and that that's what
makes up the play.

The power of the word that arises from consciousness
and contracts into an expression and form became so
absolutely obvious to me as I wrote the section on the
ego. I had always known of the power of the letters that
make up the words, but never to the degree that I experienced it while writing this book. After writing the
poem for a given chapter, whatever statement I made

whether it was "I am full of pride," "I am worried," or "I am greedy" would become my reality. I felt as if I was swimming in this world that I had painted on paper. I understood that every letter is not just a letter, but also a mantra that defines our reality. I experienced the deepening of the realization that all we are is pure consciousness. The power of the mind and the ego, and the attendant identity with the thoughts and feelings, is awesome.

I felt as if I had been given a paintbrush to paint realities, whether painful or joyful, and then I'd live in these made-up realities for a few hours until I remembered again: "Oh yeah, I'm just the painter. I forgot!" When I remembered I was only the painter and not the painted, I returned to joy.

I began to see joy as part of a sacred circle in which we are always able to rest until we decide to grab one of the thoughts rolling around in the collective mind. Then we can become lustful, worried, full of pride, etc. Once this occurs, we are stepping out of our circle of oneness and separating in order to play out whatever thought form we've grabbed. It might be comparable to leaving the palace as the king and then putting on different costumes and identities. We may look like a beggar, thief, or monk, but we are still the king. Similarly, even when we are in our contracted forms and believing the limitations formed by the letters, which create the words and then the identities, we will still be pure consciousness.

There is so much power available to us – more than a million atomic bombs. If it were used consciously, we would become beings that our minds could not begin to conceive of at this time. Love would be felt by all of us at all times. But this is a *Play of Consciousness* as Swami Muktananda termed it in his spiritual autobiography of that title. The saints say that nothing can happen that God doesn't allow, even the negative forces and separation that we have just explored. Everything can take us back to God if our intention is to know the truth and if that is God's will. Every negative quality that we have thus far explored in The Door Closers can be another doorway to the Divine, as it is all consciousness. Even the negative power is part of God's play and is a reminder to return home again and to imbibe God-like qualities in order to evolve our soul. Just as a tree grows very strong roots in a climate in which the weather is harsh, we too may evolve more quickly in the adversity that we may experience in this body. The saints all say that to attain a human body is the greatest gift and that many souls are lining up for this experience because of the degree of evolution that is possible here. In his book, *The Tibetan Book of Living and Dying,* Sogyal Rinpoche speaks about this very thing:

> "Every spiritual tradition has stressed that this human life is unique, and has a potential that ordinarily we hardly even begin to imagine. If we miss the opportunity this life offers us for transforming ourselves, they say, it may well be an extremely long time before we have another. Imagine a blind turtle, roaming the depths of an ocean the size of the universe. Up above floats a wooden ring, tossed to and fro on the waves. Every hundred years the turtle comes, once, to the surface. To be born a human being is said by Buddhists to be more difficult than for that

turtle to surface accidentally with its head poking through the wooden ring. And even among those who have a human birth, it is said, those who have the great good fortune to make a connection with the teachings are rare; and those who really take them to heart and embody them in their actions even rarer, as rare, in fact, 'as stars in broad daylight.'" (23)

It is only while in a human body that we are capable of having the many and varied experiences that are not available to disembodied souls. Part of the Earth journey is to forget so that we can again remember *who we really are*. Using everything in our experience to return us to God is one of the greatest accomplishments of our human life. In the play of consciousness, shifting from small mind to the Mind that we all share and remembering all that we have forgotten, can continually unlock the door to the Divine. This simple shift can return us to the Oneness by reminding us that we are all of the same essence.

Ego Purification

Our biggest ego problem arises from the belief that we are separate from God. This false belief causes us to identify with our bodies, or the costumes we are wearing, instead of with our soul or God self, the One who is wearing the costumes. Undoing such false identification is not an easy process. When we remove the costumes, we can feel as though we are pulling off something that has been glued onto us for a very long time. When the costume comes off, it hurts. But it is our ego that is hurting, not the true Self. When our ego is cleansed, all that remains is God. Many contemporary spiritual teachers teach that purification of the ego is unnecessary as we already are "That." At the absolute level of reality, this is true, but at the relative level it is not. *A Course in Miracles* integrates these two opposing positions with the words, "Miracles are everyone's right but purification is necessary first." [24]

I have witnessed many people, including me, experience an awakening to the absolute Reality but because of a lack of ego purification and hence a lack of spiritual maturity, they become arrogant and overconfident. Rather than embracing everything and everybody as one, such an attitude only serves to isolate them from others. Even if we have had an awakening, in most cases, there is still more work to do on the ego. Purifying the ego, so that we can experience true humility, is a long and ongoing process. Spiritual teacher Andrew Cohen, founder of *What is Enlightenment?* magazine, speaks of this in an interview in Berthold Madhukar Thompson's book, *The Odyssey of Enlightenment:* "They are not able to carry enlightenment in the only way it is meant to be carried, which is to get nothing from it for oneself... when the ego is tamed, one cares about the evolution of consciousness as a whole." [25]

We must begin to recognize and purify the ego that keeps us separate from God and from others. We must identify ego when we see it, and be willing to cut it down at its root before it creates a reality. We must notice those moments when our ego jumps in and wants to take credit for everything we do, think or feel. As we consciously and regularly work on ourselves, we must also observe our pride and remoteness from others and from life. This process of purification is somewhat like trying to tame a wild animal.

Witnessing all of our ego reactions and not acting on them becomes a very important task at this time, as we are emptying our container to be able to hold more Love. This is when we need to get out the magnifying glass in order to examine our every thought, word, and action so that we can begin to treat others better as we practise seeing them as God. This is also a time when a truly enlightened master can be of immeasurable assistance in directing and freeing us from the snares of the ego that covers our true Self so totally.

The process of striving to consciously improve ourselves can go on for many, many years. But a time may come when our efforts become a path of struggle and no longer bring the grace that they once did. Having become tired and therefore more receptive to God's will, we may be ready for the next step. In his book *Spiritual Awakening,* Sant Darshan Singh addresses this very point: "Ultimately, to reach our final goal we will have to surrender. There is no way out - sooner or later we all must come to that stage. It is just a question of whether we take a long time or come to it straight away... Once we have surrendered, we have won the game of love. We become the Beloved's, and the Beloved becomes ours." [26]

The Christian Mystics speak about the upper school of purification of the ego. Even when one has been able to train the mind not to grab the thoughts and is able to rest more inside and move beyond the senses, we still may encounter some hidden separations of which we are mostly unaware. Pride runs deep and can create an identity of importance out of anything. I remember hearing a story once about Suso, a 13th century Dominican monk who was greatly respected for his purity and his wonderful teachings. Everyone loved him for his joy, which emanated from his spiritual state. One night, Suso had a prophetic dream in which he was taken by an angel to an upper school of learning and told that he must undergo some difficult trials that would purify him of his weakness and pride so that he could be one with God forever. After this dream, Suso spent many years in a deep depression as his life became increasingly painful; since he was an artistic, sensitive mystic, he experienced these trials more acutely than most. Then one day, a desperate woman brought forth a newborn baby and told everyone that this was Suso's baby. He was a celibate so this was seen as the worst possible crime. But when Suso saw the child, he knew that he could not turn away from it, even though it was not his. Instead he accepted this child's arrival as God's will. Hence, the intense purification of the upper school continued. Everything that Suso had thought himself to be was challenged. All of his good merit left him and he was socially ostracized as a feeble, lowly person, in contrast to the great monk that he had once been. He was forced to live in the city and deal with all of the accompanying pain, dirt, noise and poverty. These trials were hard on Suso because he had become highly sensitized from all of his intense spiritual practices. His life became impossible, he complained all the time, and he could no longer practice anything that he used to preach. All of his years of self-flagellation and meditation were useless. Eventually, he "lost it" entirely and felt no connection to God. Realizing that he had been a fake, he knew that he didn't have the strength or the faith that he had thought he had. He observed pride in himself that he hadn't been aware of before, which reduced him to a blubbering, helpless baby.

Finally Suso reached the nadir of pain and began screaming and crying in the streets in agony. After he cried himself out and calmed down, having witnessed all of his human frailties, he totally submitted to God's will. It was at this point that he passed the final exam and God pulled back the curtain to reveal more Love to him than he had ever felt in his whole life. Suso then received a vision that he had reached the end of his trials. His humility was complete. He knew then that he did nothing and that God does everything. All of his talents meant nothing as they were the ego barrier that separated him from his complete surrender and union with God. In the end, Suso returned to the world to do God's work in a much deeper and more compassionate way than ever before. He was beatified by Pope Gregory XVI in 1841.

This final surrender is the purpose of the purification of the ego. According to 20th Century Christian writer and teacher, Evelyn Underhill, "Human pain is the price; the infinite joy peculiar to free souls is the reward." [27] The final purification is a deeply human process in which we are asked to leave the light and face our human darkness. The spiritual self can no longer be seen as separate from our personality self, which does not fully embrace God.

One might ask, "Why would one need to go through such an intense purification process?" Such a process is actually a state of grace, in which the deeper coverings over the soul begin to be removed so that the light that we are can shine with its entire splendor. The ego identities crystallize inside our beings, and create hidden separations, of which we are mostly unaware. We can only accomplish so much by observing the ego patterns with our conscious minds. At this final stage, we are propelled beyond the limits of our minds in order to undergo a higher level of purification, which will lead to a greater spiritual maturity.

The Yogic scriptures speak of these deeper ego impressions of which we are consciously unaware, as Samskaras, or scars in the soul. Samskaras are impressions left by our past thoughts or actions forming our mental and emotional conditioning. These are stored deep in our being. It is often difficult to witness them, as they have become such a large part of our ego identity. This is why we attract certain events, people and situations, which in turn trigger deep reactions that serve to loosen this solid identity structure. It could be compared to breaking up cement to reveal the pure earth beneath.

As long as we believe that we create our reality, our ego remains intact. When we believe in our own personal power alone, we can live a very long time enjoying the personality and ego self, alongside our spiritual practices, believing that we have arrived. The spiritual energy can feed and support our ego life and it can feel quite full and complete.

Then, one day, things may begin to change. Loss of career, health, parent, child, or anything to which we are deeply attached and identified, can bring us to our knees before God. Life can seem to take on a will and direction of its own, as we watch the dissolution of our ego-based self-image and all of its attendant desires and supports. As our perception of a solid world crumbles, we may feel as though we are grasping for air as we watch things melting away. We may feel as though we are dying or that we never existed at all.

At this stage, some people go into therapy to try and figure themselves out, and some are able to successfully
make some kind of transition. But more often than not,
therapy tries to reinforce their old notions of themselves, rather than help them to die to their ego selves,
or to let go and welcome the release of a life that no
longer fits. Those who had found refuge in their spirituality may experience a loss of the bliss that they once so
easily accessed. At this stage of the spiritual journey, we
may feel as though the bottom has dropped out of our
lives and we have been left to wander in a spiritual
desert. This may cause us to feel frightened, guilty,
doubtful, and to wonder what we did wrong.

When we begin to come into fuller consciousness, we
must fall out of our concepts of what life is, what spirituality is, and what our place in it is. To know the Self
directly, we must die to all the old ideas, concepts and
images; we must empty the container, so to speak, so
that we can fully embody the truth. Then our whole life
becomes a spiritual experience.

Here life takes us into some difficult passages, so we can
learn true humility and we can experience our connection to all other beings and life. This is where we must
give back God's "toys," such as psychic and spiritual
powers. Even though we may feel that we have faced
and purified our egos, we must trade in our earlier rap-
tures or illuminations to allow the deep, dark, dormant,
and previously unknown parts of ourselves to appear. It
is here that we are welcomed to The Dark Night of our
Soul. In this passage into maturity, we will face our powerlessness and we will come to realize that we never
truly did anything. Not a breath was taken, or a movement made, without God's Grace.

Part

4

The Journey Beyond The Doors

But the faith and the hope and the love
Are all in the waiting
And do not think
For you are not ready for thought
So, the darkness shall be the light
And the stillness the dancing

T.S. Eliot

Again, the Being of Light from the far away galaxy asked God, "What journey do these beings have to go through to abandon ego and separation?"

God replied: "After a while, the beings who had been driven naked from the garden realize they are not happy in the realm of darkness, separation and fear. They also realize that none of their ego drives and desires can ever fulfill their true needs. They come to see that their awakenings and dalliances with the Light, and the inconsistency of the open door, only increase their longing. None of it is enough to return them again to the garden. Nothing they can do out of their own strength has any true power.

Some of them have the courage to enter the darkest nights of their souls. Here, all the hidden demons rise up to cleanse them, freeing them from duality and separation once and for all. Since fear is deeply imbedded in their minds, there are many difficulties, challenges and tests they have to face in order to disengage from the identities they had previously believed themselves to be.

Sometimes in this passage, the pain and pressure becomes very intense, and they might feel like jumping out of their skin. But they now know to cry out to me for help, whereas before they would just despair. Like drowning men and women, they cry out from the depth of their souls, begging the Light, disguised as darkness, to reveal itself and to relax them so they can take another step through the dark fog, where all previous brightness is hidden from their sight. These souls are totally dependent on their Divine Self for every breath, for they have given away their ego power in order to enter the dark doorway to the Divine. They risk everything they thought they knew, for that which is as yet unseen and unknown."

To Enter the Darkness

To enter lovelessness, for the sake of love
To enter forgetfulness, for the joy of remembering
To enter terrible loneliness, to know all Oneness
To enter into darkness, only to discover Supreme Light
To enter and believe doubt, guilt, confusion, and fear
Until one day the veil is removed to reveal perfect Love
To cry the soul's tears of separation
And to grieve and long for something formless
Until these very tears transform themselves into Divine Nectar
Replenishing and renewing the broken heart
And to grow so tired
Of believing, hoping, or trying to be anything
That the nothingness becomes the place of supreme peace
And then, to return home, to that which was never left
Fuller, wiser, and filled forever
Never needing to look away again

The Dark Night Of The Soul

T here is a beautiful story in which Narada asked Lord Krishna to show him the nature of maya or illusion. Krishna sent him to fetch some water. On the way, Narada met a girl, got married, had children, and lived that life for many years, until a flood came and he lost everything. As Narada wept and grieved over the loss of his family, and all that was important to him, Krishna appeared and gently said to him, "Narada, where is my water?" Upon hearing Krishna's voice, Narada remembered *who he really was* and understood that nothing else had ever happened.

Krishna had shown Narada the nature of maya. When we enter the forgetfulness of The Dark Night of the Soul, we are fully veiled to our true nature, and we experience the pain and sorrow that accompany the forgetting. God in the form of maya concealed Narada's true Self so entirely, that Narada's sense of loss and abandonment were complete.This story reminds me of Vivien Leigh, the actress who played the desperate and neurotic character of Blanche in *A Streetcar Named Desire*. Leigh played the part so convincingly and became so identified with Blanche, that she could not return to who she had been prior to taking on the role. For quite a while, she believed that she was Blanche and eventually had a nervous breakdown. Not unlike Vivien Leigh, we can get caught up in the various roles that we play on a daily basis, believing ourselves to be a particular person who has a particular life, when in fact, that life and that person are simply illusions.

A friend once told me about a dream in which he came across a coat rack, took down a mask from it, and slowly placed it against his face, watching the eye holes coming nearer and nearer. Then, to his horror, he realized that he could not remove it and that people began to relate to him based on his mask. He cried out, "But this isn't me, this is only a mask!" But they persisted in treating him as the mask, and so he forgot his original nature, and began living an illusory life.

This is why we walk through The Dark Night of the Soul, so that the mask can be removed once and for all and so that we can live in our true nature. The Dark Night of the Soul is the gateway to a higher state of being. The purpose of the dark night is to free the soul to become Reality itself. For this to happen, the very core of our personality, created in accordance with the outer world's vision of life's purpose, gets challenged. All the loves, desires, and dreams that we have held dear get shredded. Until we reach a deeper understanding, this process can leave us feeling unhappy and confused. The deep negativity in the personality is such a compelling polarization of our previous spiritual illumination that the old negative personality seems to be our predominant reality. Feeling as though we have moved from the infinite and into the limitations of the finite, we can wonder if we have ever experienced spiritual illumination at all.

Although unique to each person, The Dark Night of the Soul can give rise to boredom, emotional fatigue, illness, depression, fear, and a sense of being dead to life, in both spiritual and worldly terms. We can often find ourselves unable to use any of the previous techniques we had learned to transmute darkness into light. In discovering that it is impossible to purify ego with ego, all previous levels of understanding are challenged, leaving us without a solid foundation. Compounding this, we may perceive the world around us to be unsympathetic to this kind of transformation, thus amplifying our sense of unworthiness and powerlessness. Confusion and doubt may set in if we compare our experience of the ego being removed to others whose egos appear intact if not larger. Just as some of the mystics suffered great physical trials in this stage of purification, we, in our modern culture, have our own brand of suffering. While centred in the mind and emotions, our suffering is equally painful.

When we are in The Dark Night of the Soul, the distractions of the outer world can amplify our self-doubt, our need for approval, and/or our loss of faith. Feelings of confusion and unworthiness are magnified tenfold by the polished pace of the outer world, especially in those areas for which we still seek external approval. This can create a great deal of suffering. But over time, and after much breaking down, we become disinterested. There is a sense of being removed from life as we've known it, somewhat like a death.

If we could immediately empty ourselves of spiritual or worldly identities, there would be no need for the dark night. Indeed, the ground would be open for the remaking of a new being. Unfortunately, very few have realized God totally; few can hold the enlightenment experience without first going through a strong stage of purification. The dark fire that burns the seeker's last vestiges of ego is a necessary burning so that a new form can emerge, based on a completely different foundation.

In the end, we will come to see the emptiness of all that we have learned from the many therapies, techniques, and concepts we have adopted, and from all that we have read and been taught to believe. We will realize that our many attempts to visualize a better or improved life is like moving the furniture around in a room that remains unchanged.

To do anything or become anything at all, even enlightened or liberated, is just another concept. Finally, when we fully feel our powerlessness, when we tire of our stories and our concepts, and when we feel exhausted from the purification journey, then we will cry to God from the depth of our soul, with an open, shameless heart. Then we will be ready to experience the True Life - the Life of Surrender, of Love, of Presence – where no doors are ever opened or closed.

The phrase, "it is always darkest before the dawn" echoes the process of this dark night. In the beginning stage of ego purification, each time a part of the ego is dissolved, our lives grow sweeter and knowledge increases. The Dark Night of the Soul is different in that it is the final surrender to the God Self, the only all-pervading Reality. All sense of doing and separation which had previously felt comfortable, become unbearable. This transformation might be comparable to the contraction a snake feels when it is time to shed its skin. Similarly, there comes a time in the soul's life, when opportunity knocks on the door. Such an opportunity may be disguised as divorce, loss of career, loss of spouse or family member, childbirth, menopause, illness, injury, or just an inconsolable grief springing from a bottomless well within.

The mystics say this grief of the soul comes after tasting God's grace and joy. But, in the life of the spirit, there are no prerequisites for experiencing different stages of growth. For example, the great 20th century Indian sage, Ramana Maharshi, experienced complete enlightenment through his terror of death and his accompanying recognition of the impermanence of his body. Others have pierced the veil of illusion through severe hopelessness. Still others may have such conviction in the truth, they maintain God consciousness throughout all their trials in life. For many of us, however, it seems to be a slow grinding down of the small ego self, during which time happiness and outward joy seem far away. Even if we have never read a spiritual book prior to our dark night, when the time comes for the soul to drop its previous sense of identity and to merge into living life from the God Self, the rules no longer apply. We are all spiritual beings in human form, tasting desires and experiences, until, after many lifetimes, we are summoned to awaken, once and for all.

The difference between Hell itself and this stage of soul darkness is aptly described in Dante Alighieri's *Divine Comedy*. Dante (the main character as opposed to the poet), is a flawed individual who has taken the wrong path. His love, Beatrice, no longer alive, asks the Virgin Mary to help Dante see the error of his ways. Mary intervenes by sending Dante on a three-day trip through Hell, up Mount Purgatory and finally to Heaven. At the outset, Dante is spiritually lost and so he meets guides who help him press on forward. His principal guide through Hell and Purgatory is Virgil. Once he struggles through the fog and murk of Hell, Dante climbs on the body of Lucifer and emerges into another kind of darkness and approaches the threshold of the great mountain under the stars.

There comes a time in our spiritual lives when we are required to live for a time in purgatory, where we will be unable to see anything outside of ourselves because the smoke from our inner fire veils our eyes. As long as we seek to escape from our various hells and to free ourselves from pain, we will remain bound. We can emerge from the pains of hell in one way only, and that is by accepting the suffering, which is seen as purging rather than meaningless damnation. The souls in The Dark Night of the Soul suffer the same torments as those in Dante's Inferno. But with willing accepance, instead of bitter resentment, they recognize this process as a meaningful and necessary passage, thereby accepting responsibility for their suffering. This is the only key that will open the door.

Facing and taking responsibility for this pain is particularly difficult for one who has experienced beautiful states and has been a positive and uplifting person. But the ego has not let go of its identification with the person who experiences these wonderful states of consciousness; it still has the pride of attaining something. There is still a doer left, and although the person has made great strides toward goodness and love, and may have great understanding, there is still a separation between the God Self and the small self. It is because of Love that lovelessness arises. The previous identities of spiritual awakening and joy are therefore replaced by anger, loneliness, guilt, doubt, abandonment and black, unspeakable thoughts.

A number of well-known mystics speak eloquently of the suffering of The Dark Night of the Soul. Saint Angela of Foligno, a 13th century Christian mystic, said: "I would have chosen, rather, to be roasted, than to endure such pain." [28] Meister Eckhart said: "It's as if there were a wall erected between Him and us. The I, which, looked upon eternity, has closed. The old, dear sense of intimacy and mutual love has given place to a terrible blank". [29] In his spiritual classic, *Dark Night of the Soul*, the 16th century Carmelite monk, St. John of the Cross, writes:

> "That which this anguished soul feels most deeply is the conviction that God has abandoned it, of which it has no doubt, that He

> has cast it into darkness as an abominable thing,
> the shadow of death and the pains and torment
> of hell are most acutely felt, and this comes
> from the sense of being abandoned by God,
> being chastised and cast out by His wrath, and
> heavy displeasure. All this, and even more, the
> soul feels now, for a terrible apprehension has
> come upon it, and thus, it will be forever. It
> also has the same sense of abandonment with
> respect to all creatures, and that it is an object
> of contempt to all, especially to its friends." [30]

During the Dark Night of the Soul, it is not uncommon to experience a complete loss of the former self, including gifts, abilities, or powers that had seemed to work up to this point. Poverty, illness, inconsolable grief, shame, and self-hatred, are shared experiences among mystics through the ages. Often there is a tremendous sense of abandonment and guilt, particularly in those who had previously experienced bliss and goodness. The seeker can't help but wonder "What happened? What did I do so wrong to fall so low?" The states of bliss present in the earlier stages of ego purification had spurred the seeker onward to keep burning away old identities. But in The Dark Night of the Soul, there don't appear to be rewards for one's efforts. Spiritual books and practices that had opened the door to the Self may appear dead and boring. Meditation may just lead to more sadness. Our interest in God, in people, or almost anything once loved, often wanes. According to 18th century French mystic Francois Fenelon, "God tasted, God felt, and God enjoyed, is indeed God - but God with those gifts that flatter the soul. God in darkness, in privation, in forsakenness, in insensibility, is so much

God that He is, so to speak, God, there and alone. Shall we fear this death which is to produce in us the true divine life of grace?" [31]

During The Dark Night of the Soul, the soul is forced to look at the darkness from which it had previously hidden. The sense of its imperfection, before the purity of the big Self, can be astounding and overwhelming; and the distance between the small self and the God Self can seem almost insurmountable. Seeing the bare truth of what lies beneath our surface personalities – the self-will, pride, need for praise, disdain for blame, anger, or needing to be seen as anything at all – becomes as apparent as looking at large ants through a magnifying glass. The hopelessness of changing any of it with one's own strength adds to the pain.

But the time of The Dark Night of the Soul can be the biggest doorway of all to enlightenment and to Love of the purest kind. It is not just a smattering of spiritual awareness and a good life, but the dissolution of the identity with the small "I" consciousness, and the coming home to the soul's totality.

To Fall So Low

How can it be, having glimpsed your Divine form,
That I could fall so low
Lower than the lowest vermin
Oozing with the poison of the ages
Into a dry, lifeless land, where no love exists
And decay prevails?
Forgive me for my sins
I knew not what I was doing
Even so, if you wish me to die, I gladly will
But my longing for you can never be killed.

The Fall
From Grace

After having many deep spiritual experiences, profound healings, and even accumulating some powers, I felt happy with myself and with what I thought I knew. I felt a kind of trust in my God Self, as it seemed to be so alive in me. After my first enlightenment experience, I lived in a deep state of constant bliss for about a year. During this time, when things that I valued were removed from my life, I found myself laughing at the losses, as I felt very protected and held, as if I were in the arms of God. Why should I worry? I was aware of my ego that was in need of purification, but I still believed there was a me that all of this light was going to enhance somehow. Spiritual materialism became my reality. I craved my experiences of light and bliss. I was confident that I could just tap into myself and transmute or erase my problems, or that I could meditate and experience love and peace. I even found that if I just used my mind in the direction I wanted to go, or visualized a positive outcome to a situation, it would happen. I had a sense of power and charisma with people. As I mentioned in the Awakening chapter, many offers came to me that were leading to fame and fortune. Just as quickly, they went away, as though blown away by the wind.

I prided myself in my lack of attachment to fame and fortune's quick arrival and to its equally quick departure. I felt I had a strong foundation, but gradually, after many years, the losses began to add up and doubt began to seep in. My foundation was not as firm as I had thought. I began to feel increasingly worn down with each new obstacle, such as financial difficulties, which gave rise to survival and health issues. I also felt undermined by the constant judgment that I encountered from my ex-husband, boyfriend, family, and friends who could not understand any of what I was experiencing. They kept alluding to my great potential that never seemed to materialize. But somewhere I knew that I was embarking on a journey to the center of my soul. Beneath the surface of my knowledge lay my hatred, jealousy, fear, unworthiness, and lack of faith, all the things that had been hidden from me before. These states began to rock my concepts and I even began to question my faith in God. The pain of moving through this dark time became so intense that I no longer wanted to live. I felt like Icarus, who had flown too close to the sun and then had fallen into the harsh reality of the limitations of the body. This was very difficult, for I had developed a strong identity with my soaring self. What happened? What did I do wrong? Why did God abandon me?

After years of spiritual practice, sitting with Masters, experiencing Love, and what had felt like lifetimes of purification, I found myself unable to think even one good thought. One day I could no longer rise above my pain. I felt I had done something wrong, that my connection to the Divine had disappeared. My faith was shattered. I felt abandoned in a black hole, and I had to face my deepest darkness. I had to face my fear of the impermanence of the body. I had many thoughts of death and my hope for a future life vanished. A number of friends and family members were sick and dying at that time as well, amplifying my sense of nothingness and powerlessness. I realized that out of my own strength or will power, nothing could be done to change any of it. All my attempts to change or improve myself were useless. Each attempt was more useless than the last - a difficult lesson for a "doer." I had spent years trying to be healthier and happier, but nothing worked. Because I didn't have a confidante who understood this journey, I was frequently very hard on myself. My relationships only reflected my sense of unworthiness and incompleteness.

I could not look at magazines or watch television, because it all seemed to be endless inflated images of eternal youth and joy. I felt as though I was dying while everyone else was allowed to live, make money, look good, and have a life. I hated all of it. To make matters worse, I judged myself so harshly, and felt so guilty, I decided I was a complete failure at life. Naturally, everyone I met would reflect back to me my belief that I was a failure; hence, I erroneously saw them as confirming these beliefs. Even in the sanctuary of my meditation center, a friend said to me, "Too bad you don't fit in here very well." Other devotees looked so full of the life I used to feel coursing through me, believing what I used to believe about Love. I felt like a grey, walking corpse. I understood the plight of sick people and the elderly; I understood what it is like to die to the body. A friend of mine did die during this time. Sitting with her before her death, she expressed to me the same feelings that I was having. We were in the same space, even though she was leaving and I was staying. Death without leaving seemed horrifying.

I stayed away from most people because their judgments only increased my doubt, fear, and guilt about what was happening to me. My sensitivity level had grown to a state of extreme discomfort. The doctors had labels to explain my physical illness. Some suggested I go on *Prozac*. But, despite the pain, deep inside I knew I was OK. I knew there was a larger purpose for my suffering, for I was touching a part of life that needed understanding. I was willing to go through this dark time unaided by drugs, even though the juice of life had left me. I remembered how, in my earlier bliss states, I would pray and ask for total union with my God Self, thinking this would mean more vibrancy, more trophies, and more spiritual sensory stimulation. Had I known what was in store for me, I may have been more careful what I was praying for.

My ego was truly unhappy. I felt as though I had turned into a horrible person who hated everybody and everything. My pain arose from not understanding that my

doing and achieving, the very things that the world reinforced, were ineffective at this stage. I slowly began to
realize that I was being asked to surrender my self-will
to Divine will. I had to discover how helpless I was on
my own, even with all of my so-called personal power.
In realizing that I was still identifying myself as the person to whom this was happening, I began to grasp that
I did nothing without God. As my life slowly changed,
much of the time I was exhausted and sad as I watched
the subtraction process of my "self" taking place. Any
desire I had to be somebody or to get somewhere was
blocked somehow, forcing me to give up and rest in a
deeper part of me. Not having any high experiences or
positive feedback seemed boring at first. But over time
"blissed out" became "blissed in" and I came to prefer
the still, quiet space of my God Self, to the exciting,
hope-filled way of living in my ego self.

My desires became simpler. I had less need for conversation; my mind and others' minds held little interest.
Healing therapies or just about anything that spoke of
improvement felt dull and conceptual. I began to see that
no matter how much people figure out their past lives, or
their emotional and mental tendencies, in the end it's like
playing with illusory images on the movie screen of life. I
saw that we all live in our own movies, desperately performing, crying out for a positive response from someone.
When that response doesn't come, we suffer. All that we
are really asking for is to be seen in our divinity, but our
egos turn to the wrong channel and misinterpret that
desire. Trying to get anything from the human ego realm
was an endless, endless job.

Even if we try to be happy, positive, and virtuous, we are

still just moving marbles from one side of the mind to the other. There is no real change; ultimately it is illusory. Over time, I became increasingly disinterested in the outer reality. Compassion grew but it no longer reeked of syrupy sentimentality. It was the only reality that was true. I finally realized that I am not here on this earth to get something; I am only here to use this body to know God. With that realization, the door began to swing open, and an awareness of the Divine in all things started taking over my ego-based life.

You Frighten Me So

You frighten me so
You look like the most ugly monster I could ever
imagine
I don't want you near me
Your presence makes my skin crawl and turn cold
Yet, you chase me relentlessly
Leave me in peace
But you laugh demonically and grow uglier and larger
To escape your tyranny, I must run faster but I stumble
and fall
Heartbroken and tired
I cannot run any longer
"Who are you?" I ask
No answer
Who are you?
"What do you want?!?" I scream
No answer
Finally, terrified and defeated
I turn my face to you and gaze into your eyes
And in great surprise, I see my own Divine Self
Reflected there

The Demons

After my first direct experience of *who I really am*, I had a life-transforming dream in which I was asked to be in a garden fashion show. I was given one important instruction: "You will walk through the garden and then you will reach a black woman sitting at a table, and she will tell you to turn left." This seemed quite clear, so I began my work in a joyous state of mind. The garden was beautiful, sunny and uplifting, with many exquisite fragrances. I felt vibrant, alive, and attractive in my lovely clothes. I continued feeling this way until I reached the black woman at the table, which was barren, with no decoration at all. She gave me a severe look and pointed to my left. I felt disturbed but I was ready for anything. I started walking to the left and found myself in a dreary, misty, grey area, void of any colour. As I looked closer, I saw that a steely grey barbed-wire fence defined the path. I began to feel fear and discomfort. Everything felt dead as it crunched beneath my feet. I really wanted out of there; this place was beginning to terrify me. An icy chill ran up and down my spine. I knew I had to do my job, so I kept going, but my fear increased and I started to sweat in my lovely dress. I felt even more contracted, since the clothes did not belong to me.

Picking up the pace, I finally reached the end of the path. As I turned to go back, everything that had crunched under my feet became demons that looked slimy green and evil. They had hatred in their eyes as they tried to tear at my face; I felt as though they were going to kill me. By now, I was beyond terror. I didn't know what to do or where to go, so I kept walking. Then, a loud commanding voice inside me said, "If you give those demons power for an instant, they will kill you. They are not real. They are only illusions." The demons came closer. "You can't hurt me. You are not real." As I said this, they softened and dissolved into thin air. Each demon looked scarier than the last. My only power was to see them as unreal and harmless, and to keep going. Finally, soaked with sweat, I reached the entrance to the garden again. I stepped into the lush, green beauty, but everyone, including the black woman, had disappeared. As if I'd just left a battlefield, I fell on the ground. As I lay there, a tremendous peace, strength, and sense of maturity welled up inside me, making me feel ancient.

This dream has been a great life teaching. As well as an omen, it was a gift to guide me through the journey I was about to undertake. As I entered the deep darkness of my life, many demons presented themselves, and I have not always been as adept at recognizing them as I was in my dream. Sometimes, I have been immersed in some of the dark thought forms, emotions, and mental states, and have suffered as a consequence. The demons have come in many forms – illness, grief, others' disapproval, projections, guilt, fear, doubt, abandonment... Whenever I haven't listened to my inner knowing and have become caught in the outer play of appearances, the demons, which feed on fear-based beliefs in separation, arrive and I suffer. Like opening Pandora's box, if I make the unreal more important than the real, I am drawn into a whirlpool of demons. I have come to realize that the demons are really here to show us where we need to be strengthened. From this powerful, archetypal dream, I have discovered that instead of running away or resisting or fighting the demons, I need to look at them and examine the gifts they offer. Everything in our lives, including the demons, has but one purpose: to free us from separation and to open the door to our true home, which is eternal.

✤Meditation Keys – The Demons✤

⚷ *Recall a recent moment in which a demon has appeared to you and thrown you off balance – a self-doubt, a self-judgment, or even a judgment from another person that has hurt you.*

⚷ *Take some time contemplating this demon and then ask yourself, "Am I believing this demon to be real and forgetting my true Self?"*

⚷ *What is the gift that is being offered here and how are you being strengthened? For example, self-doubt may be taking you to self-trust, self-judgement may be taking you to self-love, etc.*

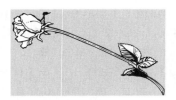

Where Did I Go?

Why have you taken all my dreams?
And all my gifts, all my strengths?
My life feels unfulfilled, underutilized and sickly.
How will I live here in this world with other people?
How will I survive?
I am so afraid and so sad
I am no value to anyone anymore
I used to be someone with energy
Someone of importance
One who could make a difference
How will I be of any use now?
Without a solid identity of control and power
I mean that's what they show on TV.
In the movies and in the newspaper, isn't it?
Isn't that how it is supposed to be?
Is there even a place for me on this earth anymore?

The Shattering of The Worldly Heart

To enter The Dark Night of the Soul is a Divine gift. It is a time when the soul faces the deep unknown within itself and finally purges itself of lifetimes of misunderstandings. Nonetheless, there can be great aloneness at this time. In this age of "fast food" spirituality, passing through this period of transformation with trust and acceptance is a great challenge.

Adherents of some Eastern religions make preparations for this passage for many years, but as contemporary seekers, we want instant results. This makes the passage particularly hard, especially if we are inclined to beat on ourselves for being in the stage of ego death for what may be quite a long time.

Disengaging from identification with our ego personality is more easily said than done. In my experience, the loss of ego felt like the greatest loss I had ever encountered. The pain of the soul cuts much deeper than any emotional pain. I could not believe the depth of my sorrow. I felt as though I had died and left my body, yet was still walking around, relating to others, and feeling their projections upon me, as though I were still there. It was a kind of torture, perhaps comparable to being in the bardos, a term given by Tibetan Buddhists to realms of passage between life and death. Inhabiting two worlds while still basing my worth on my former life was painful.

All I had known myself to be, all my dreams, fantasies, concepts, loves, and passions, were erased, not to be replaced by anything my ego liked. I was in a deep depression; I felt as though I had nothing solid to hold onto. I didn't want to wake up in the morning. I clung to the belief that this dark journey was an important step in my spiritual life, but eventually I even lost touch with that notion.

Disinterest grew and my heart longed for the old life and the people in it, but I was being pulled further and further away from the world I had once known and enjoyed. The little pleasures I had once loved seemed hollow. I was in a constant state of fear and my heart felt shattered. I told people all kinds of lies so they would leave me alone and not try to fix me; I told them what I thought they wanted to hear so they would feel comfortable with me. I pretended that my life was normal, much like theirs, and avoided telling them what was really going on for me because I didn't have the energy to deal with whatever reactions and judgments they might have. I found it difficult to look anyone in the eye for fear that they would find me out. It felt odd to be someone devoting my life to Truth but needing to lie just to survive.

It was the ego mind that was giving me such a hard time, since its conditioned commentary on my situation was heightened. I had believed the commentary to be real, based on concepts of how I should be, or should feel, whether in the world, or in my spiritual life. I slowly watched as my results-oriented, so-called personal power slowly dissolved into the higher power of "Beingness." This process challenged everything I knew myself to be. Eventually, I saw my depression in a whole new light. Having looked upon my state of not caring as a bad, unhealthy thing, I came to realize that depression was Divine Grace's gift to me. By pulling me from the outside to the inside, from the unreal to the real, I was being carried to the only place where I could find a little peace. I began to understand the meaning of the Sufi teaching – being in the world but not of it. As I began to understand a little of the process, the Divine door would open and a waft of light would temporarily pour through. In those moments I was truly grateful for the shattering of misunderstanding.

✱Meditation Keys – The Shattering of the Worldly Heart✱

Whatever state you're experiencing during this stage, however it feels, see it as God coming to you in that form, and allow yourself to sink into it, as if you were sinking into the heart of God.

Standing Before God

Humility is the doorway to the secrets of the heart.
Humility knows the "I" is an illusion,
knows it's a smoke–and-mirrors affair,
endlessly struggling to project an appearance of
solidity.
Humility means seeing our lives as games, our games
as trivial,
our triumphs as temporary.
It means abandoning, here on the prayer mat,
all that we thought that we were and knew.
If we want to know the meaning of humility,
We might search out the strength of the servant –
Not the whining, complaining servant –
The strong, willing one whose strength comes of
helping others
And in serving a Master who shines with the light of
a million suns.

A Sufi Prayer

Humility

Humility before God is one of the fruits of this time. During the dark night we have the opportunity to see our pride, our judgments of others, and our self-righteous sense of right and wrong.

As we begin to learn true humility, we become aware of the boxes and categories into which we have cast others whom we judge as right or wrong. Since pride is so hidden in our natures and so strongly supported by our culture, if we do have a job, money, security, or even a spiritual path, we take it for granted that everyone else should be just like us. Those who fall short of this identity are collectively seen as having done something wrong. Very few of us take the time to understand how and why people are as they are, and thus our pride remains intact, unchallenged by life.

The Dark Night of the Soul challenged my judgments of good and bad, right and wrong. I found myself in situations

I would have never dreamed of in my previous life. The person I had thought I was, was dissolving. Money seemed unattainable, no matter how hard I worked or what I tried to do, thus shattering any belief I might have had that my previous good fortune had been my doing. Illness struck my previously healthy body, and I had to stop working. As a result, I found myself lining up to collect a monthly welfare cheque with all the people I had previously judged. At first, I felt shame, but after a while and much breaking down, I cared a lot less about what others thought of me.

During this time, I felt as though I was opening my door to misfortune from which I had previously wanted to run. My father and some close relatives passed away, a close woman friend died of cancer, a couple of other close friends were teetering on the brink of death, and two friends committed suicide. Another friend was looking toward me for support with her drug and alcohol problem, while another, who was down in her luck, was asking me for money. I spent many years taking care of an elderly woman until she passed away. Needless to say, all of this was overwhelming. Dealing with so much hardship enabled me to see my judgments and how much I needed to grow, to love myself and others, and to see beyond appearances to the true beings that we are.

I used to impose spiritual concepts upon myself and upon other human beings who just needed love. I gained a fresh appreciation that to truly see God is to love unconditionally. Being unhealthy allowed me to understand the fragility of old age and disease. I would notice how young people would briskly cross a road without concern for an older person whose every step was shaky. I noticed how much New Age thinking lacked humility and compassion, as someone's misfortune would be chalked up to karma, or the belief that they had created their own reality. The shallowness of these beliefs became very evident to me. In fact, I began to realize that I had no idea how anything worked; I could no longer come up with a formula or accompanying lingo for anything. All I knew was that I didn't really like what I was experiencing and seeing in myself. I would often pray for forgiveness for the multitude of sins I witnessed in my mind every day. I had become an unimportant person in my eyes; I didn't believe anyone would take a sick welfare recipient seriously.

We give such power to labels and images, no wonder it is so painful to lose our identities without first establishing our inner Self. I saw the delusion in our collective conditioning and the need for us to fall from our pedestals, so we can extend ourselves to God with a cup emptied of self-importance. With humility, we can begin to understand that it is the Creator who orchestrates every tiny occurrence, not the ego. With humility, we are awestruck by the Love available to us at all times, in all situations. The sense of vulnerability that remains enables us to merge with God, like fire with dry grass.

✤Meditation Keys – Humility✤

🔑 *The next time you judge someone who is going through a dark time, ask yourself the question, "Where would I be if all of my comfortable props were stripped away?"*

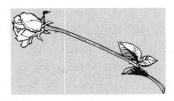

How Can I Forget You?

You looked at me and touched me deep
In the center of my soul
It felt like a blazing fire
I felt weak all over
As if your look would dissolve me
How could I ever forget you and your love?
How am I to carry on?
It's as if you've imprinted me
Branded me, then abandoned me
With nothing left but this curse of fire and longing
I cannot hear or see beauty
Without the pain beside it anymore
Nothing is left but your bittersweet love

The Longing

As the darkness descends, the pain of our longing for the Divine grows. As we are pulled away from both worldly and spiritual delights, we are left with a longing that permeates every cell. Sometimes the longing takes the form of loneliness or deep sadness. Sometimes it manifests as a physical ache or burning in the heart or belly. Little by little, our desire for worldly things begins to disappear leaving us wondering why anyone would want to stay on this earth. Incurable illness has been known to take over at this time. In her time of longing, Mirabai, the great poet-saint of the 16th century, wrote: "How can I live without Hari, oh, mother? I have gone mad. I am like worm eaten wood. Medicines and herbs do not work on me because my ailment is divine madness for the Beloved." (32)

Madness, disinterest, a sense of loss, separation or abandonment are all characteristics of longing. Just as a lover pines for his/her beloved, a person in longing for the Absolute Truth, or God, can think of nothing but that moment of merging. Longing is one of God's greatest gifts to us. Most of us would prefer not to have this gift, as it gets in the way of our lives and our happiness. But cloaked in this intense pain and desire, is a sweetness that surpasses all else. My longing took the form of a lamenting lover of God. My body would ache with sexual desire that I was not even interested in fulfilling with an earthly man. Consequently, I was highly irritable and could not bear people, noise, or demands of any kind. I no longer wanted to be in the world. I lost all interest in career, in friendships, or in cultivating outside interests of any description. I would watch myself speaking to people through a dark grey haze as I tried to interact and pretend to be interested. I was so bored with my personality, I could no longer play the game. My only thought was, "Take me home so I can lie in bed and feel God's Presence wrapping Itself around me." Each morning, as I awakened to the alarm, I would hold myself and beg to feel the Presence around me. I had to numb the pain each day with some kind of exercise in order to maintain some semblance of being an interested human being. Keeping up this façade, however, became very difficult.

Food tasted like wood. I wore the same clothes nearly every day, unless I had to go somewhere. Then, the struggle of changing and dressing was tremendous. I did not want to be bothered with one more thing. Everything that had to be done, felt like a great struggle. A persistent energy pulled and tore at my heart. The only way I got any relief when out in the world with people, was to complain about the weather, PMS, menopause, my health, their health, anything that would relieve the pressure from the searing, burning, madness in my body, mind, emotions, and soul. Then I would go home and cry and beg God for forgiveness for my whining and my inability to withstand the pressure. Everything looked dark to me, even if it was bright outside. The sun was unbearable. So was the rain. Nothing felt comfortable. I desperately wanted to be left alone, but noise, traffic, demanding people, and money worries were unrelenting. Around others, I felt intense loneliness, like a deep, dark emptiness in my body. All of this suffering seemed to have but one purpose – to intensify my longing to completely merge with God forever.

This longing is a great gift, if we can recognize it as such. It will make us want nothing but absolute absorption with the Divine Lover. Like a demon that won't rest until it has entered the magic doorway, the longing will focus all parts of us to bring us to this Union once and for all.

✣Meditation Keys – The Longing✣

Identify something for which you have a deep longing.

Take the person, place or thing away from your focus and simply feel the longing itself.

Let the ache in your being lead you to immersing yourself in the One Great Heart.

Just When I Think

Just when I think there's something to get
You snatch it away from me
Leaving me with the starkness of 'what is'

Just when I think there's something to give
You dissolve the object of my giving
Leaving me feeling inept and powerless

Just when I think I'm on the verge
Of believing myself to be something solid
You blow away my reality
As if it were a mere cloud

Just when I think I've followed
What you want my life to be
You change it all
And make me wonder
If I've heard your messages at all

Just when I think you have abandoned me
In the cold nothingness of unknowing
And the pain becomes too much to bear
You turn around with the greatest tenderness
And fill my empty cup
With the sweet nectar of eternity

Confusion

nce I was immersed in the dark night, the confusion began. I encountered a number of people who appeared to have a lot of answers. Some had studied scriptures, some knew psychology, some had studied with Masters, some were accomplished numerologists and astrologists, some were schooled in New Age philosophies. When my life began to fall apart, I received everyone's New Age or concept-based understanding of what I was experiencing. I was told I had lost it all because I didn't feel deserving or because I had some deep blocks that needed hours of rebirthing sessions. Others advised specific crystals or cleansing programs. Yet another friend said that my troubles would end if I received an initiation from a Master who was doing something completely different from what I had previously experienced. I was advised to read Deepak Chopra and to get into my body to clear issues around my father. It was suggested that I change my mind and change my life. Some teachers said tantric sex would transform me. I was surrounded by people who enjoyed teaching me, yet if I tried to express a feeling, I'd be cut off and they'd continue talking, as if I hadn't spoken.

I began to realize that my story was not going to get heard at all. All of the well-intentioned advice and guidance only reinforced my doubt, rather than supporting my true Self. I felt as though I had messed up and had failed miserably.

This sense of not being heard or acknowledged extended into the physical realm. Every naturopath, homeopath, or acupuncturist, had a different diagnosis. Every doctor I went to, except one, diagnosed a new disease or advised me to open up to my spirituality. Hairdressers colored my previously perfect hair either orange or gray, to match the gray I was trying to hide. I watched my hair fall out, at which point hairdressers would say that I was lacking silica or B vitamins, both of which I was already taking in great quantities. Drycleaners shrunk my clothes. Nothing in my life seemed to work. I kept trying to fix it, but to no avail.

I would go to psychics, and would feel uplifted for a day from receiving positive news or being told that I was somebody great in a past life. Then my own knowing would kick in and I would recognize that none of that would help me now. Vitamins and diets didn't work. Crystals, ceremonies, and most "healings" didn't do much, unless the healers had lost their acquired concepts and were really with God's Presence. I sometimes got caught in the myth that many "spiritual teachers" were professing – that we were in a "new" time of spiritual awakening in which purification wasn't necessary.

When I bought into that belief system, I would resist my deeper knowing that what I was experiencing was a requirement for my growth and not a mistake. I kept trying to control what was happening with the support of many others, who felt that my circumstances could be changed, and it was my responsibility to change them. I just had to find the proper formula. It is confusing to live in a time of spiritual materialism in which we can manifest whatever we wanted, and "spirituality" is just another way of satisfying the senses, attaining powers, making our lives nice, and being seen and acknowledged by others. I was told that if I just meditated or spent enough time with my Guru, I would experience great sensory delights. The opposite happened. Seeing the emptiness in everything that had worked for me before, I just grew more depressed. Everything felt fake. Nothing I could do was going to have any effect on this pain. I felt remorse to realize how much pride had ruled my spirituality and my life. My need to be seen and recognized in one form or another had just transferred itself to my spiritual life. I saw how weak my foundation was, that I could be so affected by self-doubt, judgment and fear.

The confusion scrambled my apparently solid reality. Anything I thought I had understood was no longer valid. Others' teachings or concepts became meaningless words. Nothing made sense. One and one no longer equaled two. Feeling out of control and helpless, I sought therapy, so I could express some of my confusion and loss. I discovered that many therapists dive into the content of the situation and try to rearrange the story or make sense of it, in some linear, palpable way. Some go into the past, which at times felt like an endless well of issues that could never be resolved. I observed that many therapists were identified with their own body/ego, so how could they help a person who was in the midst of breaking down that very structure? The only "therapy" that could ever work was one in which the light and presence of the true Self would dissolve the false belief in my identity with the story itself. One unexpected and unwanted development during the dark night was a state of celibacy, which went on for years. This challenged my identity more than anything else. I had been a model and a dancer for many years and had associated my power and creativity with my role as a woman and as a sexual being. I was held captive by collective, ego-based consciousness, fashion, and by men's response to me and my role in the game. Later, I realized that part of my journey had been to dive right into the sexual game of believing that I was the form, in order to know it intimately, to gradually understand it, and to finally become free of it. I came to understand how we can be caught by the magazine images that reinforce a lower level of consciousness. We are taught to see each other for what we wear; for the size of our breasts or penises; for our hair, eyes, teeth, shoulders, buttocks or legs; for how much money we make, what we drive, where we live, what we do and so on. Through this difficult celibate period, I felt as if I had been cut right out of the movie, right out of the magazine, so I could get a higher perspective of the illusion that we take for granted as being meaningful.

In reading Alan Watts' *The Taboo against Knowing Who You Are*, I learned how difficult it is for all of us to wake up to our true nature. In our culture, we have very little support for the growth of real consciousness and Love - the very things that would make us truly happy. When we look at others or ourselves, we don't see Divinity. We see money, breasts, or faults. We only see from the limited self that loves only its selfish desires. How could there not be war and greed on this planet? The changes that we think are so revolutionary and the great technological advances are little more than moving the furniture around from one century to the next, cloaked in present-day designer packages, yet seething with greed, hatred, fear, jealousy, anger, pride, and antiquated, mammalian-driven sexual programs. Nobody sees the truth, the formless Love. Our only choice is to die to these beliefs and images and emerge as God. Only then can anything ever change.

Seeing the futility of resisting the breakdown I was experiencing, and confronted with my inability to do anything in the old way, I slowly began to give up. Something much greater was in control. The gift of all the frustration was the capacity to live in the true Self that needs no one else's opinion or direction. Through the grace of God in the form of confusion, I was being led to *who I really am*. The confusion slowly exposed my identity as a woman who was rich, poor, happy, sad, healthy, sick, smart, stupid, spiritual, worldly – as the duality that it is. When I finally relaxed into my confusion, the door swung open to reveal God's humorous Love. This whole play, when seen from an elevated perspective, really is quite absurd and funny.

✤Meditation Keys -- Confusion✤

🗝 *Identify something that is currently confusing or challenging you in your life.*

🗝 *Instead of struggling with it, stop, be still and let your deepest knowing come forth.*

🗝 *See the confusion as God re-routing and opening you to surrender to the divine Self.*

The Great Death

I picked myself up from the mud
Like a warrior who has lived through the battle
So deeply tired I was, but strangely free
The fight with all its missiles and guns and fire
Had been my ally all along
Not the enemy I had once thought it to be
There was no battle
Only one long parade of lies being killed

Why the Death?

hy the death? This was a compelling question while writing this section of the book, and I spent a lot of time contemplating it. Eventually the answer came: "So that the life of the ego can become the life of God. So that the life of despair can become complete trust in the universe. So that the foundation of fear can become the foundation of Love."

In this phase of the journey, identifying with form becomes identifying with that which is formless. A life of bondage becomes a life of total freedom, in that the soul is finally released from the belief that we are a limited form that lives and dies. We now know that we are eternal and deathless, that we are the entire universe, not just a little speck of sand. We die so we can return again to the garden that has been patiently awaiting us. The death is the end of sorrow, the end of doubt, guilt, and fear. How can we doubt when there is no longer a doubter? How can we fear when we have become our eternal nature? How can we feel guilty when there is no longer duality – no right, no wrong, no good and no bad? How can we be confused when there is only Truth?

In abiding with the struggles of our bodies, minds and souls in this death process, we can know all other beings' struggles. Spirituality is not a cold ascent into the light, but a deep understanding and compassion for the perfection of every tiny little piece of Creation, whether it is perceived by the mind as dark or light. Spirituality means seeing all that is in form and all that is formless as God. Then there is no longer a split, no longer duality. Just an "is-ness" that cannot be analyzed.

Why must we go through this dying if we're already free? Because most of us are profoundly identified with form; our belief in what we see with our physical eyes is all-powerful. But what we see, what we feel, or what we think is not necessarily what we are. Our physical eyes can see only that which is impermanent, that which dies and changes. All of us are heavily invested in that reality. When death does approach, or when we experience the loss of a career or relationship, we experience terror. We believe we are this form alone, and we need to hold on to what we can see for fear that it will disappear. This belief in limitation and separation is where war and all the sins of mankind originate. The magic doorway takes us to the potent world of the unseen, to the presence of our God Self.

To break our bondage with form is to die to our identity with a limited self that has no faith or trust in anything that it cannot see, feel, touch, or think about. To know God is to know pure, vibrating Love that swallows up all problems, fears, and doubts. We may be so bound in heavy chains of belief that we are just a body, mind, and ego, and so burdened by our physical concerns that we are unable to fly. But our wings have not been clipped; they just haven't been exercised for a long time.

The dark night frees us once and for all from suffering. Even though being held down or held back from our former comfortable and successful ways feels like torture at times, such limitation makes it possible for our souls to soar into space, into eternity. It makes us understand our reason for taking on human form, so that form and formless can dance as one. Then, and only then, can we truly be all that we came here to be. Only then can we become the open doorway itself, to all who are ready to enter.

Sweet Sorrow

Surely I must be mad
This grief tugging at my heart
And tearing at my belly
Feels so strangely sweet…so rich
I must change this
I cannot allow this to be
Yet, it calls me home
To the deep, dark
Peaceful stillness within

Grief

As we watch our old self die, not to be replaced by anything for some time, as far as our limited vision can determine, we discover grief as an intrinsic part of The Dark Night of the Soul. This grief can feel like loneliness, deep in our hearts.

I was in continual grief during this time. I was often "spaced out," not wanting to face life. The losses were many and the pain was constant; I felt as if my life could not continue. The day my father died, I sat by a pond and sobbed from the depths of my soul. I was crying for myself, for the loss of my father, and then, as I experienced a deeper grief, I found myself crying for the entire world, for all of the pain that we experience, just because we are human. My grief turned into a prayer to the Creator, an offering of the separation we all experience.

After my prayer, I felt strong hands take mine and hold them. Not only were they connecting me with the

Unseen, but they were showering blessings of Love on me. Instantly my grief was transmuted to a great joy. I knew in that moment that grief was actually another form of God loving me. I saw how we all need to surrender our hopelessness, pain, fear, confusion; we all need to get out of the way and allow the magic doorway to open to eternal Love. Then we become the Love that can shine, unencumbered, to all of life.

✤Meditation Keys – Grief✤

Take some time to recall your most recent experience of grief.

Let yourself fully feel this grief. Feel where it sits in your body and how it tastes. Notice how it makes you breathe. Notice how your heart, hands, back and belly feel. Spend some time exploring the physical sensations of this grief.

Remove the label, "grief," and all attendant thoughts about your experience of grief. Allow yourself to breathe more fully into this state. Feel the raw feelings and sensations as the Love of God that is pulsating in you and caressing your soul.

Trapped am I

This stiffness in my muscles
This gripping in my stomach
This dryness in my mouth
And these horrible pictures of annihilation in my mind
What is this all-pervasive substance called fear?

It smothers me
It dampens the fire that arises in my heart
And in an instant, it can turn my world of beauty
Into a world of demons.

I have held on so tight for so long
that I might stay alive
But this is not living

Grasping tightly doesn't seem to change life's mind
As to which way it chooses to go
So I pray that you help me relax and flow
Into the love that will lift me so high
That this substance called fear
Will become just a distant memory

Fear

In The Dark Night of the Soul, fears crawl out of nowhere. I had always considered myself to be quite fearless and have taken pride in taking big risks. I even used to get handfuls of speeding tickets. But when I encountered the deeper nature of fear within my psyche, I was shocked and embarrassed at how extensive this fear was.

After a particularly difficult meditation retreat, I took a walk on a below-zero November night. As I walked by a house with smoke billowing from the chimney, I felt warm inside. I looked at the cozy little house and imagined the people resting in comfort. Suddenly, before my eyes, the house disappeared, leaving only an icy, stark, barren lot. I was shocked, but when I looked again, the house was back. Such a vivid experience of the illusion and the impermanence of form touched a deep fear within me, and left an indelible imprint. When I returned home, I ran to my apartment to see if it was still there. Everything in my world became temporary, including me. I learned that there really is no security in this world.

I became afraid to cross the road or drive a car, for fear of death. I felt as though I could watch my own body dissolve right before my eyes. I feared people; I couldn't look at them. I felt everyone's thoughts and feelings. I did spiritual practices to try to chase away the fear, but the fear only intensified. I became so sensitive, I felt as though my nervous system had become a radio receiver. For a long time, I felt everyone's unexpressed fear. It was only when I realized that I was experiencing the primal fear of death, which exists in all human beings, that I could relax and observe it from a different perspective. I wasn't going to get myself out of this state by analyzing it or by using my will. I saw that I was not the fear and that God had taken the form of fear itself. I then asked myself, "for what purpose?"

I came to understand that fear is the absolute expression of "doing," ego, and/or separation. All fear can be traced to the fear of death of the body because our identification with it is so deeply imbedded in us. Its symptoms manifest as fear of anything that can be "lost," such as our safety, career, relationships, health, youth, or money. It can also take the form of fear of judgment from others, or fear of losing our good character in the world. Ultimately, we fear the death of the identity in which we appear to be clothed. Believing that "I am this body/ego/personality" is our greatest attachment, and yet to know *who we really are*, this belief must be dissolved. This dissolution is comparable to a physical death.

As the purification process progresses, and we get closer to true surrender, fear is used to expose more of our ego. The more we hold onto the belief that we make anything happen, the more afraid we will become. Just as a boil must be lanced, we must be cleansed of our fear in order to rest in a new foundation of Love and Trust. When I could see my fear as God, then I could relax and allow the true surgeon to do His / Her work, for I knew that on my own I had no power to make the metamorphosis from human to Divine. Surrender meant letting go of trying to make fear go away.

The intensity of the fear drove me to beg God to reveal to me the state that surpasses fear. The answer I received showed me that I don't really live in this body, or in this world, in the way I had thought. I was doing laundry and feeling very contracted, afraid of how my life might or might not work out. Then I looked around the laundry room and saw its dreariness in a new way. I looked at the ceiling and felt as if I had floated up to it. In that moment I realized that I was not limited to this form. In fact, I was not limited to any form at all. I just "was." Then, everything around me became like a dream, and I, the observer of the dream. The body was a dream, and so was this life. The true "I" could never be afraid. My fear came only from believing that this costume, called Devrah, was permanent. When I saw how truly eternal and all-pervasive *I really was,* I could relax and my fear could become peace.

✤Meditation Keys – Fear✤

If you find yourself feeling fearful, do not judge yourself.

Breathe and remove the label, "fear" from your experience and relax into the feelings and sensations that remain.

As you relax into these feelings and sensations, see that what you had labeled as Fear is God coming to raise you up from the impermanent body to the Eternal.

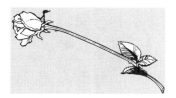

I Can Struggle No More

God – if I'm not worthy to be who I am
And feel what I feel
Then call me a sinner
For I can't try any more to be good
Righteous, caring, strong, spiritual and disciplined
I cannot work at being something
Other than what I am right now - in this moment
I cannot continue this role that depletes me
And leaves me without real, ongoing Love
When will it be enough?
I feel love when I can rest in myself naturally
Performing for nobody
When I can listen to the quiet song of a bird
When I can sit and just hear the silence between the
lines
The lines have become so tiring to me
I have not the strength or the interest
To engage in them right now
If there is more struggle required to open the door
Then it will have to stay forever closed
For the trying has come to an end for me
For surely I must be worth
More than all my trying

The End
Of Trying

O nce the grieving and the hopelessness reached an all time high, I was no longer willing to try to attain a higher state of awareness. I couldn't see the point of going somewhere to be uplifted for a few hours, only to return to the same old mind patterns that were part of my normal life. I was angry. I was finished with chasing Truth and fed up with the struggle. I wasn't willing to take another step to open this door. In fact, if it stayed closed forever, then, fine! What was I going after anyway?

The end of trying, the end of striving, the end of trying to control the Grace of God, the end of guilt, the end of virtuous conduct for the sake of attaining something... We usually reach the end of manipulating and using techniques to take us to that which is already here once all resources have been exhausted.

When we are still "doing" spirituality or "doing" a life on our own steam, our cup of water is full and there is no more room. When we begin to realize that all of our efforts have been a game to keep the cup full, then and only then are we ready to empty it of our doing, analyzing, and struggling. When we no longer care about attaining anything else but what exists in the moment, we can finally rest, and our cups can begin to fill with the true, natural nectar of the God Self that we've always been, despite all the form-related ideas our minds might have conjured up.

One afternoon as I lay on a bench looking at the sky, feeling an effortless sense of peace and stillness, not-feeling any need to pursue anything, a flood of awareness came through my being and I was shown my whole life, as though I was just passing through. I saw that the tiniest thing that happened was necessary. I was just a passenger, not the driver. All the things that I thought I had done, good or bad, right or wrong, were perfectly orchestrated. And I really did not have to worry or feel guilty about any of it. It was all going to happen anyway. All I ever needed to do was simply watch the dance without becoming involved. I saw that my suffering came from my belief that I was the one who did it or needed to do it, whatever the "it" was. Whenever I needed to make some kind of move, the "Force" would have me move. The message was, relax and enjoy the show with detachment.

I understood what was meant by "being in the world but

not of it." The answer to any questions of worthiness I'd had became clear. If I'm alive and breathing, then that is enough. My worth does not come from anything I do. My worth is what I am. "I am" is enough. With this realization, the door can effortlessly open to reveal deep and profound contentment.

✣Meditation Keys – The End of Trying✣

Imagine yourself in a room with dozens of doors that remain closed, no matter how hard you try to open them. Each door represents a desire to experience something other than what you are experiencing now.

Instead of trying to open the doors, relax. Take this closed door situation as a message to align yourself with the Self that reaches beyond all doors, opened or closed.

Let go and let God.

Love is the Sculptor

*This pressure is so strong; there is nothing I can do to
relieve it
I try so many things, to channel it or move it
But it is relentless
It feels like Love's hand is on my body, mind, and soul
Pressing on the raw clay of my life and sculpting it
Into a pure expression of
God's own life*

The Final Push To God

As the dark night progresses, we may experience a great pressure building in our mind and body. All previous ideas of watching the mind and managing it through meditation seem a gentle, distant memory. Our outer life often becomes very difficult.

It seems as though God uses whatever seems to most upset and irritate us, to take us to the final surrender of our sense of "doing." In my case, the pressure took the form of illness, extreme sensitivity to noise, breathing difficulties, and the stress of trying to meet the needs of people around me, including friends who were dying, but without the energy or resources to do so. No doctors, naturopaths, chiropractors, or physiotherapists could alleviate my painful symptoms. Constant rain, harsh sun, and loud music exacerbated the pain.

Requesting anything from anyone seemed highly complicated, and I would find myself desperately pleading like a crazy person for insignificant things. My nervous system had reached a point where one more bit of stress or one more demand from anyone would drive me mad.

One day, I lay on my floor weakened and depressed. I just lay there and asked the Creator, "How can I be free of this pressure?" Moments later I was shown the movie of my life, and saw that my desire to be free of the pressure was not the answer. The pressure was being used to free me from my previously limited self. With every cell of my being, with every breath, I remained in the power of the present moment, filled to the brim with Grace. There was nowhere left to turn, and the door I had been pounding on began to open to peace and rest.

✤Meditation Keys – The Final Push to God✤

🗝 *Envision a recent time in which you were completely overwhelmed by the pressures of the day.*

🗝 *Allow yourself to relive the intensity of that time.*

🗝 *As you feel the pressure mount, instead of fighting with it or trying to get rid of it, see it as the hand of God nudging you toward your true life.*

🗝 *Notice that when you stop fighting the pressure, it can take you to sweet inner bliss.*

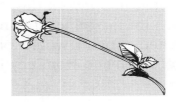

Go away!

I hate it when you pull at me
For I have nothing left to give you
I need every last drop for myself
I can't do it - I can't open up the way you want
I feel as if I am going to shatter
Into a million pieces
I resent your need and judgment
And I am angry at your demands
I must take something for myself
And rest in this quiet place alone!
So please just go away
But, as I rest, my hands become luminous
And my heart expands and light pours through me
Unblocked - not only to you
But to the entire universe
Surprised, I see how I've never lacked anything
In fact, I've had more than I could carry
So it needed to be given back from whence it came
To free me from this burden of anger and resentment

Anger and Resentment

nger often surfaces in the dark night. The door seems so difficult to open, and the energy, pressure, and irritation in the body create such tension. I had always thought of myself as a relaxed person, but during this time of purification I became a demon who wanted to spit poison at everyone just because they were alive and breathing. Old resentments surfaced. My rage toward the world intensified. I had no patience for others, especially their stories, and especially if they were trying to draw strength from me in some way.

Some of this was good. My boundaries became well-defined. My intuition became clearer and I could see through lies and manipulation more readily than I had before. But my anger weighed heavily in my heart. I hated God and all of Creation. I resented having to keep going in a world in which I didn't want to live.

I felt victimized by my spiritual life, which instead of unfolding me and making me whole and happy was pushing me into a fire I had no interest in entering. I had been sensitized to such a degree that I could no longer function, but there was nowhere for me to be with this new energy state. I felt stripped of my earlier defenses, which had at least allowed me to function in the world.

I felt abandoned by a world that seemed disinterested and uncaring. I thought all of life was madness and stupidity. I resented people demanding even a moment of my time, since I was already walking a razor's edge to just survive the pain of each moment. I hated the body because of all the work it took to maintain it, feed it, clothe it, exercise it, clean it, get money for it, and make it sleep. One day I felt so full of anger that I wanted to rip apart my apartment and throw and smash everything in sight. In my fury, I screamed out to my God Self, "I can't do this anymore! Please help! Please help me!"

That day happened to be my birthday and I was about to go out for dinner, which I had been dreading, having spent all day in a state of anger. Then, about 15 minutes before leaving for the restaurant, I sat down and experienced a profound transition from the anger I'd felt all day, to the deepest, most heartfelt Love. I witnessed my heart become a vehicle of light that emanated forth to the entire world. I felt as if all the souls in need were drawing from me like a great magnet. I felt so fulfilled and complete. I saw that intense states such as anger and resentment can serve as birth canals for Truth; the Truth does not get revealed until it is ready. I learned also that Love is either contracted or expanded, and even in the form of rage or anger it is the same energy. Sitting there, allowing the energy of Love to pass through me, I felt all limitations clear as I expanded into the open door of the one Heart.

✤Meditation Keys – Anger and Resentment✤

Think of a person toward whom you feel anger. Allow that anger to rise up within you.

Allow yourself to get really angry. Express it fully in front of a mirror as if you were speaking to that individual.

When you have finished expressing the anger, stay in front of the mirror. As hard as it may seem at first, tell this person all of the things that you love about him or her.

Keep doing this until you feel the Love arise in you.

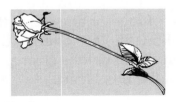

The Final Shadow of Darkness

The Devil, he has stolen my soul
And replaced it with a cardboard collage of
empty images
How have I let myself be seduced into this hell again?
He is relentless and uses everything he can
to ensnare me
My doubt, my desire, my fear and my innocence
And then he pretends he is God
And in my longing I give my power to him
And he laughingly takes all of it leaving not
a drop for me
In desperation I remember the authentic and gentle
touch of God
And I pray, with what little I have left, to be lifted
Soon I am soothed by God's sweet fragrance
And blinded by the brilliance
that removes the darkness

The Dark Age of Man

Considering the impressive scientific advancements in our world, it is hard to believe that we are in an age that is cloaked in darkness. But these very advancements can shroud the light of truth. In this time, lies seem more powerful and charismatic than truth. The voice of the ego seems far more convincing than the voice of the inner Self. Outward appearances draw us like magnets and decisions are often made out of our sense cravings.

This is why we suffer so much when we are trying to know the Self. Doubts are our greatest demons. On the surface we are living the same life as those with no apparent interest in God, the formless reality. They may seem more charismatic and able to speak about many subjects quite confidently. This can make us doubt our own knowing, especially if it isn't firmly established.

Maya can either push us toward the true Self, or it can cause us to drown in our own darkness. This dark age of man, called Kaliyuga in the Hindu tradition, has been foreshadowed for centuries. Kaliyuga is said to be a time when many souls can be liberated by speaking or singing the name of God. On the other hand, they also more readily fall into the delusions of the ego because of the powerful, all-pervading illusion that supports it. During this time, the outer appearances can seem to be truer than our heart's knowing. This confusion not only arises in the everyday world, but in spiritual communities as well. Any time we give over our power to an outside authority, no matter how good it looks, we give ourselves over to Kaliyuga. Thus, this journey is not one that is easily walked without the help of a true teacher or guide.

We always know when we've "sold our soul to the Devil." The Devil has been used as an antagonist in many religions for good reason; it is the part of us that turns away from our God Self and puts the focus on form. This turning away is also the root of much illness. I once sat with a Master and witnessed people being fully healed from life-threatening diseases because they placed their focus on God, rather than on their bodies. I've known healers who were able to exorcise people of demons or the "Devil." Such "evil spirits" only appear when we see ourselves as separate from God and as the doer of actions.

Our only salvation in this time of darkness is to turn our

face to the Creator, to the God Self within, and ask to be guided and shown the Truth of *who we really are*. This takes tremendous vulnerability, which is the source of our true power. We must speak to the God Self as if speaking to our best friend, and expose ourselves, admit our fears, confess our ego games, speak our hurts, share our loneliness and shame – honestly and without pretense. We must allow the burning and the cleansing that occurs in our hearts, as we are made ready for the merging of our will with Divine Will. Then, our breath will become the breath of God. Then, the door will open and darkness will dissolve.

Emptied by Your Gaze

I thought I knew something about God
I had experienced I was not the body
I had spent many years meditating
I thought I knew how to heal a little
How to soothe
How to speak about truth
I thought I knew something about life

Until I looked into your dying eyes that pleaded
To be released from this horrible pain and made well
I realized I knew nothing
I had no power and never did
All my learning meant nothing
Everything I ever thought myself to be
Evaporated in the moment of your gaze
And I was left naked and empty
of this burdensome identity
That has no place in the Light of God's Grace

ʃaying Ɵoodbye

With the death of my father, something fundamental changed in me. I felt as if his passing
cleansed me of parts of my ego in one big
swoop, leaving me feeling tender and childlike. I spent
a lot of time grieving him and grieving the loss of my
small self. I tried hard to put on a good front, but I could
not hide my pain.

All I knew was that what I thought was me was gone,
and what was left was an empty space. My identity had
been significantly rearranged. I also saw the incredible
gift that I received from him. Even though he was in the
final stage of Alzheimer's, I was able to speak to him as
though he were fully present. In those moments, it was
clear to me that we are not our bodies, not our diseases,
and not our problems. When I spoke to my father's soul,
he responded directly to me, even though the medical
experts told me that he had no ability to understand me.
My father's death was my death as well. My sense of

powerlessness in the face of my father's suffering allowed me to deeply understand the surrender required when we leave this world. None of the ideas we have of ourselves can accompany us in this part of the journey. One night, just before he died, the room filled with light and my dad became completely present as he looked deeply into each member of my family's eyes. Our souls connected with him in a way that had never been possible in life. It was his final goodbye. For some of us, it takes a whole lifetime just to come to that one moment of complete surrender to God. When we enter a spiritual life, we are ultimately brought to the point where we must face our powerlessness, and then, and only then, can we graciously give God back our sense of "doing" which separates us from the true power of unconditional Love.

Part

5

Returning To The Garden

*My beloved dwells in my heart
I have actually seen that Abode of Joy.*

Mirabai

*We shall not cease from exploration
And the end of all our exploring
Will be to arrive where we started
And know the place for the first time.*

T.S. Eliot

Once again, the Being of light from the far away galaxy asked God, "Why do some of these beings return again to the Garden of Love? And how do they find their way back?"

God replied: "After many centuries, many lives, many experiences, and many desires are finally exhausted, these beings become ready to throw away the shackles that have bound them for what seems like forever. When the time is right, Grace grants them the abundance of their true Being. But their lives are no longer their own, but belong entirely to me, for I am a jealous God, wanting complete attention at all times. They have become my sons and daughters who are endowed with special gifts – with constant energy, power, and love – to be used to uplift all of humanity. They have been severely tested and have had the love and the courage to take the journey. I am now in them as they are in me. Their every word is my word. Their every thought, my thought. And their every action is my action. They are the containers of my joy and rapture. Nothing gives me greater pleasure than to dance in the form I have created, where form and Formless join as one. No longer kept out by the resistances and fears of the ego self, I experience great freedom. I wait for the few souls who have tired of their long journey through illusion, to take their hands and lift them up, as a groom lovingly claims his bride. And so, we become one Being, where there is no longer form or formlessness, spirit or body, anima or animus. No…not any of this. Together, we become just the whisper that blows through all of Creation."

The End of Wandering

Exhausted and weakened
From wandering through thousands of lives
I climb the steps to meet the doorway
Expecting it to be closed as usual
Or maybe slightly ajar
On the last step, to my surprise
I discover that it is no longer a door
Only an opening in the wall
And there you are, waiting for me
As if you knew I was coming
I fall at your feet
You take my hands and raise me up
I look into your eyes
And we meet somewhere so familiar
And swim in each other's gaze
For a moment I become aware
Of my tattered clothes and tired face
That has seen much too much terrain
"I'm home, aren't I?" I ask
"Yes, you can rest now, your journey is complete"
And then you disappear into my heart
And I am made whole

Coming Full Circle

o come full circle is to realize that all of our chasing has brought us no peace. All of our concepts,
fears, desires, approval-seeking, fantasizing, and
making things happen has only made us tired of looking outside ourselves for happiness. Even after my initial spiritual awakening, I still believed I was somebody
with something to prove. In my purification, all of those
tendencies that would pull me out of the God Self were
magnified. It was a difficult journey because my mind's
conditioning was strong and supported by the collective consciousness, which has us believe that happiness
comes from attaining things and gaining respect from
others. Doubt would say things like, "You can't just stay
inside yourself and listen to those promptings. You
must do something or be somebody." Guilt would have
me believe that I was a lazy, unsociable person, for
needing the silence that is required to listen and be
nourished. Fear would tell me things like, "Look at all
the atrocities in the world. You can't trust God."

Eventually I became exhausted and disinterested enough to desire the place in which I was always happiest – the deep Self.

I once had a beautiful meditation experience in which I was falling into the most delicious inner sanctuary. I kept going deeper and luxuriating in the bliss, when suddenly my mind/ego jumped up and said, "Is this okay? Shouldn't you be doing something constructive?" Because of the joy I was feeling, the voice was a clear distortion of the truth, and I was able to recognize the ego's sabotage of true Love. I realized that coming full circle and returning to the Garden only comes after experiencing the many games of the ego. We then become bored with our ego identity and no longer believe that its voice is *who we really are*. We no longer feel bad or guilty about it because our true Self becomes the dominant reality.

Returning home means becoming free of collective beliefs about what is right or what is wrong. My own voice was developing from a deep conviction that arose like a volcano with a power that would not be controlled. Coming full circle is living inside ourselves and trusting ourselves deeply, no longer being pulled into the foundationless, unforgiving, unnurturing ego self.

In the movie, *The Last Temptation of Christ*, Jesus was undergoing his forty days in the desert. He drew a circle around himself and was told by God not to leave it no matter what temptations came his way. When Jesus saw the temptations for what they were, they would dissolve into thin air. Similarly, our temptations arise whenever we doubt or disregard our deepest knowing in favor of some external pull. Yet the resulting games and detours are nonetheless valuable. Even our crooked steps can lead us back to God. Every action we've ever taken has only been another step toward the final merging with the God Self. Our feelings of powerlessness and vulnerability have left us needing to be filled. Our pain has kept us searching. Our striving for our desires has led us to attain them, only to discover that something huge has been missing in our lives. Our hatred, jealousy, and fear have left us out in the cold. The resulting despair has pushed us onward to finally know the Love that we are. Our struggling has tired us and made us unhappy, so that in our unhappiness we have strived for the Truth. Our grieving has opened our hearts causing us to cry to the Creator for help. Our moments of true peace have reminded us of what can be. When we have felt as though we cannot take another step using our own strength, we have fallen to our knees in preparation for the supreme initiation. For the marriage to our divine Self that breathes our breath, performs our actions, lives our life, and fills our empty vessel so that we can live forever in the heart of God.

An Unending Journey

Please, show me the door.
Please tell me who I am.
Please, help me learn to see.
I will travel to India, to China to America too,
If you will but show me the real me.

I will eat very little - make myself small
And sit for hours, so still.
I will read many books - eat brown rice
And work very hard for you.
For all this I will gladly pay you lots of money too.
I will see my sad reflections and try and improve,
So I can be worthy, good and true blue.
Please, please – just tell me what to do.
Just tell me what to do.

The years go by and still I seek
Having traveled near and far.
Experiences I've had – money I've spent
Tired I am – empty I feel.
My ego battered to the ground like a fool
I've tried to be nothing – I've tried to be everything,
I've tried to see life like a school.

So smart I am now - I can tell you things about God.
It can make me sound really cool.
But something has changed
My interest has waned in self-denial, concepts
and rice gruel.

I wonder who was ever bound? Who was ever bad,
Unworthy, sad, or untrue?
Time has not improved me
Or changed anything that I do.

All good thoughts, bad thoughts
Right action and wrong action
Have brought me no closer to the clue.
So angry and flustered, I sit in this room
Surrounded by books and pictures to improve.

I am lighting a fire and burning you up
Each last strand of illusion – the fuel.
As the last strand burns, disillusioned I feel
So empty and so tired of the duel.

Just then, a veil opens and I see
I, the actor, as dramatic as can be.
So funny it is, to think I'm so important -
And most of all - a "me."
Now I can see there is no door
That is ever opened or closed-
It's just been a game I've played for a time
Until I remember I am free

When the Seeker Becomes the Finder

When we look at all the dramas and games we have played to reach the goal of the true Self, all we can do is laugh uproariously at the absurdity of it all.

When I replayed my own experiences, it felt like the most hilarious game in town. The people I met, the beliefs I tried to adopt, the lifestyles I embraced, the identities I added to my already strong identity, were fuel for a sitcom. I rebirthed myself until I was blue in the face, I fasted, and I wore clothes that were not me in order to fit into spiritual communities. I traveled to India to be with gurus, I studied with a Chinese teacher, an Australian teacher, two American teachers, one Canadian teacher, and many more in between.

I believed myself to be special for a while and then not important at all. I meditated eighteen hours a day for weeks at a time. I cleansed, I did selfless service, I did yoga, I practised tai chi, I had a huge kundalini awakening. I did daily affirmations, I watched my thoughts, I chanted, I tried to be present, I embraced my emotions, I pounded pillows, I saw psychics and channelers. I spent every penny on meditation workshops, healers, astrologers, spiritual tithing, gurus, and anything else I could think of to improve myself because I thought that I was somehow lacking. I came to see the fundamental importance of all of this searching; I eventually tired of it, which led me back to my true Self, which requires no chasing.

I initially believed myself to be the personality and ego. Then I had an enlightenment experience. But not having been purified enough, I still acted from the ego and misappropriated my enlightenment state to my body/personality self. For a time, I continued chasing after more spiritual/sensory delights until I was able to more fully integrate that experience within my being.

Fortunately I had the guidance of a great Master and support from some great teachers whom I met along the way. I played out what I needed to play out until its seeds were burnt. I was then able to return again to the place where I knew I was the true Self and not the ego tendencies. It was like having a veil removed so that I could finally be the light that I am - and have always been.

Many of us have heard the phrase, "Before Enlightenment, chop wood, carry water, after Enlightenment, chop wood, carry water." Upon our return to the garden, nothing really changes, but the foundation of life is fundamentally different. When we return home, we understand who does everything, not as a concept, but from direct knowledge. Richard of St. Victor, a 12th century Scottish-born Christian mystic, describes this process beautifully:

> "When the soul is plunged in the fire of divine love, like iron it first loses its blackness, and then growing to white heat, it becomes like unto fire itself. And lastly, it grows liquid and losing its nature is transmuted into an utterly different quality of being. As the difference between iron that is cold and iron that is hot, so is the difference between soul and soul: between the tepid soul and the soul made incandescent by divine love." (33)

Many "experts" proclaim that purification is not necessary, but in order for us to hold the Divine energy with responsibility, humility, maturity and compassion, we need to be cleansed in Love's fire. It is not about our own enlightenment; it is about respecting all of humanity as God. The only real foundation we have is in dissolving our small self into the true Self. It is only when we can see God everywhere we look that the seeker can really become the finder.

I Love You Because

I love you because you are
I love you because your dear heart and mine
Are of the same substance
I love you because of all that you miraculously are
I love you because you are a work of art
Like no other ever to be found
I love you because I need you, so I can express
my tears
My pain, my beauty, and my joy
In your precious and unique form
I love you because I Am

We Are
The Credential

A woman once asked a great Master, "Oh Lord, why should I live? I have so much pain. I have lost everything. I don't feel worthwhile to anyone anymore. Why must I still be here?"

The Master replied: "Because God needs you here. The Creator would be lonely without you."

The woman smiled upon hearing these words.

What we are is our credential, despite having learned that our worth comes from what we do. True worth, however, comes from the realization that we are already enough just because we are. We all want to change ourselves, fix ourselves; some of us even want to disown qualities we've inherited from our parents. And then we enter into some kind of spiritual life and take all of our striving for worldly things and transfer it to striving for spiritual things. Not that this is wrong or bad; it's just what some of us need to do in order to get free of the conditioning.

While going through such incessant self-improvement, there is no rest and only glimpses of truth: "Be the best you can be," "Excel," "Have goals and go after them," "Make it happen," "You create your own reality," "Become liberated." Such injunctions can be valuable at times, but because our minds externalize the self and our world, these very suggestions can have us running in the wrong direction, which is ultimately exhausting. Our true worth rests in the Being who lives our life just as it is, with all of our peculiar idiosyncrasies. This is unconditional love. How can we be accepting of others and penetrate through their ego self, if we haven't come to accept ourselves with all our funny little ways? If we haven't learned to laugh at this absurd personality we inhabit? When we accept what is, we are surrendered to God's manifestation as "Tom" or "Judy," or whatever our name might be.

I have always wanted some kind of role that would define me and make me complete, or so I have thought. But this book has been a great teacher for me. Once I decided to write it, I realized I had no box that I could fit into that would be acceptable in the world. I almost scrapped the writing of this book, thinking, "Forget it. I'm nobody. Who would listen to me?" But I came to realize that who I am is the credential, and all my struggles, joys and fears are perfect just as they are. All the mistakes I thought I had made actually led to the next understanding. I had a vision of a beautiful quilt of my life, which had all kinds of patches, designs, and fabrics. Some pieces were crooked and rough, others were smooth and even, but all pieces were important and necessary, and in their unique way they added to the beauty. After this vision, I felt a great relief. I was finally able to live my life without guilt, resting in the recognition that God knows exactly what each of us needs in every moment.

Every piece of our lives, every mistake, is our teacher. Instead of trying to escape from the person we think we are, we can relax and enjoy it, as the important piece of the quilt that it is. Then, we can see how important everyone else is, for each piece is required to make up the whole. In this place of understanding, how can we judge anyone else? We have no idea what any of us needs in order to come home. Knowing this, we can truly celebrate what we are, no matter what the outer circumstances may be. For we then can see that who/what we really are is the Love that sustains all things.

✤Meditation Keys – We are the Credential✤

☛ Spend a few moments contemplating an event that has significantly impacted your life.

☛ Spend another few moments reliving this event and how it has been a loving catalyst that has created who you are today.

Everything is You

Here I am, totally resting in your heart
But the outward appearances of your play confuse me
And get me running and chasing
For so long, I've tried to run from you
But you try to block me
By presenting me with one problem or another
Not to hurt me, or make me suffer
But to nudge me back to you
Oh, how I curse you and try to push you away
But all my pushing just makes me realize
You are unconquerable
Finally, I see - What is there to push against?
Except another manifestation of you
How can I win this game, when you are the player?
The played, and the play

There Is
Only One Power

T he true discovery in our arrival home is that there are not two, there is only one. This realization was the lynchpin that allowed me to finally come full circle. In the past, when I believed that I as my small self had to make something happen, create a life, or change bad thoughts to good, I was always scared, guilty, doubtful, stressed, and struggling. Not being the kind of person who could be at peace with partial truths, I was unable to rest until I finally understood that I am God and so is everything else.

A few years ago, I was about to board a plane to return home from a holiday. The airline had recently experienced accidents and I was afraid because we were encountering high winds. Terror arose in me, stronger than anything I had ever felt before. I tried to suppress it by eating cookies and reading magazines, but it kept building. I told my friend that I was too afraid to leave on this flight but he assured me that everything would be fine. Finally, I walked outside into the gusting wind. I said to the wind, "Please, don't let me feel separate from you and afraid." Within moments, I received a response to my prayer. I began to cry because the Love I experienced was so great. I became the wind and I became the airplane that was to carry me home. I became the mountains and the people preparing the plane for flight. From a place of beauty and peace, I saw that I am not a frightened little person. *I am all that is.* I felt the true presence of God as the one power, and I realized it could only come from somewhere other than my small ego-centered self. In that moment of realization, there was no separation between me and God. The stress, fear, guilt, and doubt were gone. As I flew home on the plane that day, I felt myself to be in a state of great peace, trust, and oneness with God. I could enjoy eating cookies because I liked them, not in order to stuff down feelings of fear. All I had to do was give up the fight and join forces with the One Power. As the finite boundaries dissolved, I could joyously dance with the greatest lover of all.

✦Meditation Keys – There is Only One Power✦

Observe your every thought, word, and action as just another manifestation of God.

Take a day and practice witnessing God acting, speaking, playing, and being – in every thing and in every person, including you.

Imagine that you are just a puppet being animated, and observe how the One Power moves you around over the course of a day.

It's All in the Positioning

Now, I really have a choice
Before, I never felt I did
But it's all in the positioning
Now, I can create worlds just with my thoughts
For I know who I am
I am free to see it as darkness, or see it as light
For it's all in the positioning
I haven't changed much
I still have desires, fears, guilt and anger
But I no longer need to believe these things
For it's all in the positioning
The mud has been loosened
So there's lots more space
To be what I've always been
For it's all in the positioning

Free To Be Me

Even though I've had some strong mystical experiences, in my day-to-day life I am the same person I've always been. My neuroses haven't changed all that much. My fear and guilt are forever cropping up. But what has changed is my relationship to these states. The mind has become much more spacious and less identified. My experiences of truth and light have gradually worn away enough of a path that I can find my way back to the true Self much more quickly than in the past. The heavy yoke of self-judgment has also lightened, leaving me freer to be who I am in any given moment.

Sometimes it seems as though I've regressed to becoming a sensitive child who feels everything and responds immediately. I am more vulnerable than ever before and often don't feel very adult at all; I'm unable to neatly control my responses and put them in a safe little box. Slowly, body, mind, and soul is becoming a finely tuned instrument for the Love that bathes me in its light, when I'm able to receive it.

How long this process will go on, I don't know. And how Love will shape me in the future is a mystery. The essence of *who I am* cannot be purified out of me. What endures is not all that different from who I was when I began, but the tough outer layers are gone, as is the belief that I am separate from God. What remains when the dust settles is something fresh and new, yet very old as well. The "I" that remains has been here forever, long before I looked out of my crib into a dark room and cried out for love. What has been purified is my belief that I am not worthy of love exactly as I am. In the absence of that belief, my desires and feelings can only be God's desires. All that is left is the experience of my form being animated and danced by the formless. Then life becomes an interesting game indeed, for we have no need to change anything within the dream. We just need to witness the dream itself and say goodbye to the bondage that would have us believe we have anything to do with whatever role we are playing. We can play our role to the hilt; it is just shadow dancing in the doorway of blazing light.

✤Meditation Keys – Free to be Me✤

Go for a short walk and be aware of how you perceive things and people around you.

Notice any and all thoughts, judgements, criticisms, or opinions as they arise on the first half of your walk.

For the remainder of the walk, see everything around you as if it were no longer you but God seeing through you.

Notice how this slight shift affects your experience of people and things in this world.

Become the Vessel

Throw away the books
Throw away your stories about who you think you are
Throw away all your therapies
Fears, identities, ideas
Break those chains. Come. Together, let's walk this
path
That very few have the courage to tread
Risk everything you are and throw yourself down
Naked and needy - become the beggar
Whose empty bowl needs only to be filled
Become the water jug, without a drop of water
Thirsting and baking in the sun
Be not content to become anything else
But the open vessel
And then wait – ever so patiently
As the vessel itself is remade into a golden human
Made of divine, ecstatic love
Be unhappy with anything else
Settle not for a few pennies, a beautiful face
Or a safe little piece of worldly property
It all crumbles and dies after awhile
No – refuse to go back to the world of the dead
Only to pretend to live in another lie
And don't be disappointed in your time of waiting
For you are not the timekeeper – you are the vessel
Waiting to hold the true riches and final destiny
Of human life

Getting Free Of The Story

Almost twenty years after my initial experience of enlightenment and the miraculous re-growth of my uterus, I was sitting on my couch reading articles about menopause and hot flashes. I felt afraid as I thought about the sleeplessness and physical inconvenience of this stage that my body was entering. I got myself so upset, I finally gave up and offered my worries to the Higher Power because there was nothing more I could do about it.

Later, I talked about this with a friend who said, "I heard someone say on the radio that what you think, you become".

Normally my ego would have been offended at hearing

a basic truth I'd known forever. But it struck a deep chord in me, and my whole journey flashed before me. This was the answer to my prayer. My obsession with menopause really brought home the truth of "what you think, you become." If I think that I am just this body that is suffering, then that will become my experience. If I know that I am not limited to this body then I am not identified with the suffering. This realization embraced my whole journey from when I was twenty-nine and re-grew my uterus to the present – in my fifties and in menopause. I understood that the journey I had been on these last 20 years has been a huge, conceptual game that I have been playing. My so-called journey had its importance, however; it taught me the incredible power of illusion, and mirrored the depth of my belief in my personal story that consisted of a past and a future.

When Krishna sent Narada for water, after Narada had asked to know and understand maya, Narada stumbled upon marriage, death, disaster, and complete ruin until Krishna showed up and asked, "Where is my water?" Like Narada, we become so attached to our individual life and story, that we forget that the story isn't real. If we believe there is a journey we must take, we will. Consciousness agrees with whatever we believe. Even Krishna once said, "My Maya is very difficult to over-come."

If there is a journey to be taken, it's only for the purpose of really knowing and respecting the power of illusion. Narada's true Self was veiled and cloaked to support the belief he was limited so that he could deeply under-stand that nothing really happened, and it was all illu-sion. This applies equally to our ideas about The Divine, so that Buddha, Krishna, God, Jesus, and whoever or whatever we project our inner Self onto, is the reflection in the water, as well as the water itself.

It is easy to get confused and believe that the reflections that we see are real. Getting free of our stories means piercing through the veil of illusions and concepts, be they spiritual or worldly. It means coming home to the true Self that has never been on a journey, and has never needed intellectual understandings, teachings, paths, or anything else. All that has ever been needed is complete silence so that the stillness of our true nature may emerge free of cloaks, masks, and veils.

But until we undergo our life journey and learn the lessons it offers through teachings, paths, and understandings, we are not open, purified, or mature enough to respectfully honour the true Self that exists everywhere and in everything. In her book, *My Lord Loves A Pure Heart*, Gurumayi said, "Impurity eclipses the higher state." (34) So the process of purification in which we believe ourselves to be everything except *who we really are*, is a journey that we all must take until one day the veils lift to reveal the brilliant light that we've always been.

In the face of such luminosity, the contraction of believing the limitations of our story becomes boring. Why would we take just a penny, when we have access to the riches of the entire universe? No matter how great a story we might think we have lived or are living, once we've experienced the highest state, it all turns to dust. If we want to create a story, then why not focus our minds on the greatest story of all, the unfolding of our very highest potential in the human form, where we no longer see ourselves as separate from God?

❖Meditation Keys – Getting Free of the Story❖

🗝 *Think of one thing in your life that disturbs you.*

🗝 *Stay with this disturbance and witness how it feels in your body, mind, and emotions.*

🗝 *Breathe deeply for a few moments until you are calm, and then rest in the space of not thinking.*

🗝 *Notice how the disturbing story melts away in the silence.*

The Dreamer

I looked down and saw a hand
Whose hand could this be?
It was attached to an arm that was attached to a body
Whose body could this be?
I heard a voice coming from this body
Whose voice could this be?
This body was a part of everything I could see
Who is it that sees all of this? I wondered
Who is wondering?
And who dreams this dream?

Waking From The Dream

At one point in my process I became concerned because I was extremely spacey. It seemed as though most of me was somewhere far away, and there was only a small part left to pretend to be the person I had once believed myself to be. Interacting with others, I felt like an imposter because I no longer believed in my former identity. I would avoid some people's gaze because I didn't feel I would be believable enough. I was not the person they thought me to be. Somehow suspecting I was in a dream, I worked very hard at concealing this knowledge in order not to appear too bland or too weird. Some friends offered solutions to try to ground me, but nothing helped. I just kept going further out.

Not fully understanding what was occurring, I felt that I must be doing something wrong. I went to doctors, chiropractors, naturopaths, etc. to see if I was sick. I blamed my state on allergies, illness, hormone imbalances, sleeplessness, fear, the full moon, imbalances arising from being a Vata in the Ayurvedic tradition - any excuse I could think of to avoid going through this transformation which was beyond my control. Eventually I realized I was beginning to live in a state that went beyond the everyday life of my body/personality. A Swami had once told me when I expressed concern about not being "in" my body: "It's none of your business whether you are in your body or not, don't worry, God is in control." This realization calmed me and allowed me to trust more in the process.

Still I often longed for the past, when I could again be what I considered to be a "normal" person who believed in herself and was involved in the world. I used to stare at people and wonder, "How do they manage to believe in their reality so completely, and operate so convincingly?" As my conviction in my true Self grew, I realized that there is nothing to strive for and nobody to become. I saw how I already was an actor in the script for the play we call life, so I let go more and more into this state. Over time, despite my resistances, the worldly longings were gone and I awoke from the dream to the True Reality that watches all of the dreams.

At a relative, everyday level, I did not change very much but my interests changed dramatically. All I wanted to do was be still or go for a walk. When I awoke in the morning or in the middle of the night, I felt as though I was waking from one dream to another, and yet neither of them felt real. I experienced quite a bit of fear because my old sense of myself was gone. However, this was short-lived, because Bliss would cradle me in its arms anytime I asked. God's love served as a reminder that I was only being dreamed and this perceived reality was not to be taken too seriously.

✣Meditation – Waking from the Dream✣

☞ *Recall a time when you awoke from a dream and experienced confusion about what was the dream and what was reality.*

☞ *Return to that moment of confusion and fully feel what it was like to forget where you belong.*

☞ *Stay with and penetrate this moment deeply. Remain with the confusion until both the dream and the so-called reality dissolve.*

☞ *Allow the Love that exists beneath it all to surface and envelop you in its sweetness.*

How can I not?

How can I not forgive you?
For I, too, have fallen into darkness and taken it to be
true

How can I not understand your grief?
For I, too, have lost lovers
And sat beside beds with loved ones dying

How can I not forgive your hatred?
For I, too, have hated from the depths of my being

How can I not understand your attachment to this
world and its riches?
For I, too, have drunk the beauty of the sun caressing
my face
And have felt my feet sliding through golden sands

How can I not forgive your greed?
For I, too, have desired the fame, the fortune, and
the glory
Alongside the frustration that arises when it seems
so far away

How can I not understand your loneliness?
For I, too, have lain there in the night
With an ache that burns through my soul

How can I not forgive you?
For what is there to forgive?
When I look into your eyes, I see the most humble
Most pure, most wise loving
being cloaked in this costume
Thinking it needs forgiveness and understanding

Forgiveness and Compassion

I once had a dream in which I was wearing big boots and play fighting with a friend. I accidentally kicked him and he fell into a deep pool of water. I tried to save him but could not and soon he died. I felt like a murderer. When I awoke, I didn't know where I was or who I had killed. Time lost all boundaries. I couldn't leave my house because I was in such a confused and guilty state. I couldn't differentiate between the so-called dream state and the so-called waking state.

Later, I meditated to see if I could clear my mind of past life experiences and the accompanying guilt. In my meditation I saw my dream from a higher level of consciousness, as though I were seeing as God must see.

There was not an ounce of judgment or blame for this experience - only compassion. The words, "You are forgiven" reverberated through my mind and my body.

Recognizing this world as a dream does not exempt us from respecting everything that comprises the dream. On the contrary, seeing one another as players in a movie, rather than as serious enemies and victimizers, enables us to let go of the anger, resentment, and victim consciousness that may have pervaded our previous reality. When we know that there is only one power and a mass expression of consciousness, we can see ourselves in every living person. When we cut even one person out of our heart by denying him or her as a part of us, we cut out all the other parts. Love cannot be dissected. Either all of it is God or none of it is God.

When we hold onto a perception of these costumes as real and important, all we are likely to experience is conflict, desire, hatred, and pride. This weighs heavily on our hearts, for we haven't accepted or forgiven others, or ourselves, and the door to the light will not open for us. Coming full circle means forgiving ourselves for our inadequacies, fears, hatred, etc., and accepting whatever part we've played in our lives. By doing this we can become fully human and can understand all others' hearts. When we understand our own motivations, whether or not they are pure, we can understand others, forgive them, and have compassion for their actions. We can look into everyone's eyes and see the untainted purity within them. The costumes we wear are simply roles that we play. When the show is over, all that is left is pure light and Love.

I have a friend, whom I love dearly, who was going through an extremely difficult time in her life. Instead of asking for assistance, she stole a large amount of money from me. When I found out, I was shocked and felt betrayed, angry, and ready to cut her out of my life. But Love haunted me, not just the human love I had for her, but the Divine Love that would not let me rest until I forgave her. One evening, I got down on my knees and offered my anger, resentment, and blame to God, so that I could forgive her. Soon thereafter, my heart exploded with love for her and forgiveness poured from me to her. I was filled with compassion, for I saw how innocent and scared she really was and I recognized that, if I had been in her situation, I could very easily have acted in a similar fashion. This forgiveness became a great blessing to me and to her. We have since spoken after many years of silence and she is intent on trying to pay me back. She asked me for forgiveness, which had already happened many years before.

From this experience, I saw how very difficult it is to truly forgive another out of our own strength, as the sense of betrayal and anger can be so strong and the idea of letting it go can feel impossible. Prayer is our only hope because it illuminates the True Self in us and in the other so we can see from soul to soul rather than simply from personality to personality.

The God Self judges nothing, but the small ego self is the harsh authoritarian that we have projected onto God for centuries. We have played God with each other, harshly holding others outside our hearts and closing the door to true Love.

To forgive means to come home, to see past the costumes, and to remind ourselves and others that we are
dreaming, that what appears to be happening isn't real.
It's just the current role. Sometimes those who play the
most difficult roles for us are those who love us the most.
Their job is to push us to awaken from the dream and
become free, and in that freedom we become the
embodiment of forgiveness and compassion.

✤Meditation Keys – Forgiveness and Compassion✤

*Contemplate whom you are keeping out of your heart or
toward whom you feel hatred.*

*Make a list of what you hate about this person and then
make a list of the ways in which you are similar.*

*Feel how these aspects you've listed have been rejected
by you. Embrace those dark parts without judging them, as though
embracing a child.*

*Allow the forgiveness and compassion of God to heal your
wounds and the wounds of the person toward whom you have
felt hatred.*

From Getting to Giving

There was a time when I thought freedom meant
I would get something
And more would be added to me somehow
And then I saw –
that freedom is the ability to give
Without reward, even when it hurts a little
And then I saw –
that freedom is the patience
That then grows more patient
Until the entire life becomes one of infinite patience
And then I saw –
that freedom is the eternal wellspring of joy
That is Self-contained in this giving and in this patience

Giving: The Eternal Wellspring of Joy

We have been conditioned to take and to fill our empty cups from worldly illusions. This leads to greed, conflict, pain, fleeting pleasures, and/or addictions. True joy arises from giving from our hearts and being truly happy for someone when they receive what they need, even though it may be a sacrifice for us. Whatever pain we feel is not from lack but from holding on to what we think we need to get. If we do not share our love and generosity, we have too great a burden to carry. As Jesus was heard to say, "If you bring forth what is in you, what you bring forth will save you. If you do not bring forth what is in you, what you do not bring forth will destroy you." (35)

Gurumayi Chidvilasananda once told a story about Baba Muktananda who was approached by a man who said, "I am very unhappy, I am just so sad. Can you do something for me, Baba?" Baba looked at him and asked, "Have you done something kind for anyone today?" The man looked confused. To his mind, it seemed clear that Baba did not understand the extent or the intensity of his suffering, so he asked the question again, this time a little louder to be sure that Baba got the point. Without hesitating, Baba restated his answer, "Have you done something kind for anyone today?" At this, the man just shook his head and walked away.

Gurumayi told the gathering that Baba had given this man a great teaching: if we can do something kind, caring, or beneficial for someone else, it will always bring us joy. Joy and freedom is not attained by getting more to add to our already full bundle, but by having the courage and the generosity to share it naturally and freely. The freedom is in knowing that all that we own belongs to the One Source, and all that we give returns to that Source, which keeps the wellspring of joy flowing.

✤Meditation Keys –
Giving: The Eternal Wellspring of Joy✤

Each morning and each night, offer all that you have and all that you are to the God Self, as if returning a gift that has been graciously lent to you.

With the same giving attitude, spend a day offering kindness, generosity, and acceptance to those whom you meet.

Extend this day of giving to a week, then a month, then a year, and then for the rest of your life.

Watch your life gradually become a life of love and joy.

The War is Over

Oh, how I've fought for centuries
My weapons were all made of angry projections
And colors of separation
I was an "us" and they were a "them"
And because they appeared different,
They needed to be changed, or killed

Oh, how I've fought for centuries
Transparent chains were tied to my ankles
And hatred and revenge clouded my eyes and heart
My mouth spit poisonous words to curse
And bring down my victimizers in my self-made prison

Oh, how I've fought for centuries
So caught in this dream of a war have I been
That I missed the golden door that was beckoning me
To peace and light
So fearful and untrusting have I been
That had all of the angels converged upon me
I would have tried to strike them down
As demons

Oh, how I've fought for centuries
I know nothing else – darkness and fear were my only
friends
I despised those friends,
Even though they were familiar

*For I wanted to be free of this cocoon made of
self-hate
Oh, how I've fought for centuries
But the war is losing its interest for me,
For nothing good ever comes of it,
and my body has not the strength
To throw one more bomb
Surely there is another way to live
Surely there is another way to be, besides
this endless conflict and pain*

*Oh, how I've fought for centuries
Yet, even though I want to end this war
Something in me fights me, even now, and wants
to keep the war alive
I do want to love, but this hate is so powerful
I watch as it grabs my heart and squeezes
the beauty from it*

*Oh, how I've fought for centuries
But the light in me is growing gradually
and illuminating the dark
And showing me my war has been untrue
And it's only been with myself
The light that is me, is pulling me up to infinite Love
And bathing me in the peace of the great watcher
Having tasted this cup of freedom,
my war is being replaced
With love, respect, compassion, for the God that lives
in my own heart
And now I can openly proclaim the war is over*

The End of the War

"Imagine there's no countries, it isn't hard to do,
Nothing to kill or die for, no religion too,
Imagine all the people, living life in peace."

John Lennon

magine a world in which we see every person as another manifestation of God. A world in which we never separate ourselves from others but recognize them as another part of us. How could war take place if we came from this perspective? Who would we be battling against? Imagine if we saw each person as another angle of a multifaceted diamond with infinite wisdom to impart to us.

We wonder why we have so many homeless, poor, or drug-and- alcohol-addicted people in our towns and cities. These people are a reflection of our separation with our Self. It takes a lot of humility to see ourselves in such apparently imperfect forms. How different the world would be if we were to take responsibility for our disowned pain, weakness, suffering, hatred, lack of compassion, prejudice, vulnerability, and fear. If we truly understood that everything that we see is our own Self, then we would take care of the aged, the disabled, the poor, the confused, the addicted, and the homeless. We would take care of and respect the differences of other countries and try to understand other cultures instead of seeing them as separate and therefore less than human.

Before the recent U.S. invasion of Iraq, I had naively believed that our world was evolving spiritually and that we had come to a place where we could work things out together. This is clearly not the case. We have not yet learned that everyone we meet is a part of God; our leaders simply reflect our prevailing lack of understanding. But our world cannot be any other way while our inner war is still raging; the outer war is just a mirror of what's going on inside all of us. This was brought home recently when I heard a friend, who had just discovered that she had cancer, blame and judge herself for having had "bad" thoughts that must have created the illness. My heart hurt as I felt that she was violating her own Self with blame. But then all of us are in a war with ourselves. We beat, blame, and berate ourselves using anything we can, be it spiritual or worldly concepts, to make ourselves wrong.

In his book, *Healing Into Life and Death*, Stephen Levine tells a beautiful story about Paul Reps, a writer and Zen practitioner who was trying to enter Japan during the Korean War in order to study at a monastery in Kyoto. During that time, non-military Westerners were not allowed entry. The Asian immigration officer told him that he could not gain entry into Japan, as he was not militarily aligned. While sitting opposite the officer, Reps turned over his Visa request form and wrote on the back, "Making a cup of green tea, I stop the war," and then handed it back to him. The officer looked at what Reps had written, considered it, and then turned the paper over and initialed it, thereby approving Reps' request to enter Japan. The officer said, "We need more people like you in our country right now."

When I first heard this story, I was perplexed, but as I contemplated Reps' statement, I understood what it means to make a cup of tea that stops the war. I noticed how much control, judgment, and violence have been a part of my daily experience. Impatience, conflict, and a desire for things to be different have often informed my day-to-day living. Even the making of a cup of tea, impatiently waiting for the water to boil, quickly grabbing a tea bag and a cup, while thinking about the next thing that I must do, is a kind of violence. Not being present in each moment is a subtle insurgence that creates the inner war. While working on this section of the book, my computer screen suddenly went black. All I had was a hard copy of the manuscript. I freaked out, despite knowing that God was taking the form of the blackened computer screen in order to teach me something important. I watched as I cursed and berated myself for not having made a backup disk of the work. I wanted to quit the whole project. I saw the inner war that I was fighting with self-blame, fear, and judgment as the weapons. But there was nothing I could do but surrender to the moment, which was when a soft voice arose from inside and said, "Maybe this is a good thing. Maybe life has its own timing for this book." I calmed down and sat for a long time just receiving each moment. In the stillness, I remembered that I have the key in my own heart to stop the war if I allow "what is" in any given moment.

If I am angry, sad, joyful or fearful, I can gently embrace what comes rather than trying to push these feelings away or blaming myself for having them. When there is no resistance, there is no war. What we are missing is love and compassion, not just for others but for ourselves and for our own fear, anger, greed, lust, pride, and other human weaknesses. If we can feel compassion for these things in ourselves, then we will be able to feel compassion for others, since we are all fighting these inner demons together. If we can begin to live our own life in self-love without warring with what we encounter internally and externally, then we can be the carriers of light in a world filled with darkness and pain. And instead of adding our own judgment and self-hate to the collective blame, judgment and self-hate, we can instead add love, compassion and gentleness for ourselves and others. This is the only way to stop the war as there will be no "other" to fight against.

We are still living in the dark ages when it comes to understanding *who we really are*. Our technology is brilliant but our understanding of ourselves and our world has not evolved much from prehistoric times.

Even people who have studied spirituality and claim to be do-gooders remove themselves from others with phrases like: "Oh it's their Karma," to get themselves off the hook from taking responsibility for their own inner separation.

After my father died, I went to my meditation center just to feel some lightness and some love. After the program, I cried as some of my grief and loss rose to the surface. One of my fellow spiritual seekers asked me what was wrong and I told her, "My dad just died." Her response was, "Oh it's just Karma, just repeat the mantra." This immediately shut me down and I saw that it is often not safe to show pain or suffering in some spiritual groups. Some devotees can be overly attached to being in a "perfect" or tranquil state, and can use the concept of Karma in a violent way, to close their hearts to the other. But many of us are so afraid of being swallowed up by another's pain and fear because we haven't faced our own suffering. In this instance, my fellow spiritual seeker struck me with the Karma concept instead of compassionately listening to my sorrow. It is true that in this realm we are ruled by Karma, or cause and effect, unless we are constantly living in the supreme and absolute state of nondoing. But if we understand that we all suffer the pain and joy of Karma while in this body, then we cannot close our hearts to anyone because we are all one.

A spiritual teacher, who goes by the name of Grace, clearly affirms this in one of her newsletters: ..."The key is that the light side embraces the dark side as the shadow part of itself, while the dark side perpetually denies, rejects and judges otherness as being outside of itself.

You are *All That Is*. That is key to this understanding. You must accept all that you are, all that you see and all that you experience and in so doing, you will experience everlasting peace. Stop fighting. Stop struggling. There is no other – and there is no other way." (36)

To come full circle and to return to the garden is to stop the war that we've been fighting, and to acknowledge that war is based on fear, whereas love is based on trust. The wars that we see in our outer world are a reflection of the wars that all of us carry on within. We are always in one form of conflict or another, defending ourselves or blaming others, whether it is the government, friends, or mates. We want others to see what we see and to want what we want, but they usually don't. Anywhere there is another who appears different from us, we become frightened and defensive and we either protect ourselves or attack. As long as we approach life from a lower state of consciousness, the wars within and without will continue. As long as we depend solely on our own resources and limited understandings, the war cannot end. When we have replayed the cycle to the point of realizing that we cannot change our limited, conditioned mind without appealing to the Divine, then we can become receptive to a life of love, humility, and peace. Once we begin to see how difficult it is to end the war even in our own self, something much greater can raise us up and we will see ourselves and others with compassion.

✤Meditation Keys – The End of the War✤

🔑 *Recall a time when you felt at war internally.*

🔑 *Notice the cause of this inner war. What were you unable to accept or allow to be?*

🔑 *Soften around this inner war. Instead of trying to change or get rid of the struggle, let yourself be at peace with it.*

🔑 *Feel the love that arises in your heart when you know that all that you are is held in God's love, free of judgment.*

Make Way for the New

Clean the closets of your heart
Make way for something clear and free of clutter
The cool, blue breeze has been blocked for too long
Make yourself ready – make yourself clean
Make yourself sensitive and receptive
Free from darkness and decay - let your soul declare
That no more rubbish will be placed here
For my appetite now is for the clearest, purest delights
And I will not be starved any longer

Removing the Clutter

Referring to the purification process, Swami Muktananda would often say that you use a thorn to get rid of a thorn, but then you throw them both away.

When we first open up to our spirituality, we may feel the need to have a lot of reminders such as sacred artifacts, crystals, or pictures of gurus, saints, goddesses, or deities. In order to remind us or to direct us back to God, we may burn incense, do yoga, sing or listen to chants, or perform certain rituals of worship. These can all serve a beautiful purpose, but we can run into difficulties when we think that these outer things are the goal and that without them we would lose our connection to the Supreme Reality.

Ramakrishna, a great Indian saint born in 1836, loved his statue of the goddess, Mother Kali, so much that he could not bear to be separated from it, even for one moment, and could not dream of ever being without it. But his soul evolution was such that in order for him to become what he needed to become, a fully realized saint, he had to let go of his attachment to Kali's form. He needed to completely immerse himself in all of the world religions so that he could know complete oneness. Letting go of Kali was indeed very painful but it ultimately freed him to directly connect with the ultimate Truth, which needs no intercessor. Ramakrishna would often return to worship The Mother Kali in the temple, but he came to her from a place of honouring God who resides in all forms. Just like Ramakrishna, we too must let go of those things that no longer fit who we are now. To be free means to have no clutter. Even the desire for freedom is clutter; it is just another concept in the mind. Direct connection to our own source is the only Truth. Anything else must use the mind, or the resources of the world of form, to stimulate our connection to our higher being. These techniques, in and of themselves, can never replace the ultimate truth.

When we reach a certain point in our development, and this usually takes many years, we become disinterested in whatever concepts that we have used to represent our spiritual journey. Perhaps we have become our own person and have found a greater trust in the deep inner self, which has been growing and strengthening. Our inner transformation may be leading us in another direction altogether, away from focusing on the outer form and more toward trusting in the formless. At first we may wonder if this is okay, having perhaps lived for some time according to the more rigid outer structures. Trusting the inner Self can seem so everyday and ordinary, unlike our former roller coaster ride of peak experiences of light immediately followed by darkness. We are simply ourselves with the same personalities; we may even wonder what all of that purification was even about. Our mind may have created fantasies about what it would be like to know *who we really are*. And our ego's tendency is to chase experiences and blissful sensory delights in order to get something to add to itself. But the reality of living in this new place is quite ordinary. Nothing has changed, yet everything is different.

While living with Gurumayi for many months, I had several peak experiences accompanied by intense burning sensations, with raging kundalini energy coursing through every cell of my body. There was an excitement when the burning would occur because I felt that I was getting rid of Karma. The peak experiences were ecstatic and addictive, and I felt like I was making real progress which could only happen while at the ashram. Once I arrived home, I was surprised to see that every stranger whom I met was as familiar to me as the people in the ashram. I had expected to be emanating light or some other spectacular sign of my transformation, but instead, I felt more ordinary than ever before. Whatever I thought I knew spiritually became a dry concept. It was no different for me to be in the world or at my meditation center. Everyone and everything seemed the same - all duality was dissolving. And I hadn't changed in the way that I had wanted to. At first I didn't like this, but over time I understood that this evenness or oneness was itself the transformation. My spiritual identity had dissolved - I was no one special. I slowly came to realize that the clutter consists of the spiritual identities that we've developed and identified with in the journey. We need to get rid of this because it tends to separate us from others who are not involved in a formal spiritual group or who are part of a different spiritual group. Since all people belong to God, we must seek to find the oneness instead of dwelling on the differences.

The teacher of an evolved disciple sent him to a great Master so that he could evolve even further. In the disciple's tradition, one was never allowed to point one's feet in the direction of an altar since God was seen to reside there, but when he arrived at the temple, the Master was asleep with his feet pointing toward the altar. Not thinking much of this so-called Master, the disgusted disciple woke him up and told him that it was a sin to have his feet pointing at God. The Master gently replied, "Well then, move them to where God is not." The disciple moved the master's feet so that they would point in some other direction only to see the altar change its position and continue to appear as though the master's feet were still pointing toward it. Finally the disciple realized the final teaching that his teacher had sent him here to understand – there is nowhere that God is not.

Coming home is realizing that there is nothing to add to ourselves and everywhere that we look is another form of God. There is no separation between the world and the spirit. We are all evolving spirits regardless of what our outward appearance might be. For in the moment of deep truth and presence, all imagined levels dissolve and we discover that we are all made of the same "stuff."

✤Meditation Keys – Removing the Clutter✤

🔑 *Spend a day watching all of the things you do to bring you closer to your God Self.*

🔑 *Spend a day not doing any of the practises that you usually use to open yourself up – e.g. yoga, chanting, bodywork, prayer, etc. Instead, spend the day pretending that whatever you are doing, seeing, or experiencing is simply another form of God.*

A Voice out of Time

There was a time when my voice spoke
Of pain, separation, anger and duality

There was a time when my voice called out
To find the door out of the dream

There was a time when my voice cried
From the depth of my soul
To have the chains of illusion unlocked forever

There was a time when my voice sang
From a great need in its heart
To become one with the Love it had tasted

There was a time when my voice fell silent and quiet
Having cried its cries and sung its songs
So, it melted into the black velvet stillness

And then a new time and a new voice arose
From the center of the earth in me
This voice was so true, and I loved to listen
To its articulate and rhythmic notes
That spoke of love

This voice was so clear
As it so gently called to all of humanity
To come join this dance of freedom

This voice was so powerful
As it cried out like a mighty mountain
And erupted hot golden lava
Onto the archaic, ancient ground
Laying a foundation for the new and yet to be seen

This voice was so pure
And its heart's essence could be heard
Singing through every thread of creation
Its vibration reweaving the very pattern of existence

And this voice - in its stillness
Seeped into every heart and into every soul
And into every voice, so that all speech spoke of Love
All that was called out for was to celebrate this Love
All cries were of joyous and boundless Love
And all songs sung of the glory and blessing
Of this nectar of Love

And when this voice paused
It had no other resting place
But the sweet, deep womb of Love

Returning to The True Voice

After chanting God's name for four or five hours, I was deeply inspired to write this section. When I began the chant, I had the usual everyday thoughts, but by the end, Divine elixir was on my tongue and "I Am" reverberated throughout my whole being. It appeared as though only the chanting could cause the voice of God to bellow forth, but I realized that when I looked closely, my every day voice had been transformed as well. I only wanted to speak of God's love; to speak of anything else bored me and I would feel dry as saw dust. More and more frequently I would witness myself expressing words and sentences that I knew were coming directly from my God Self. The chanting had amplified what was already happening subtly and naturally. I can never again take for granted the experience of God resting on my tongue and in my throat and in my heart, waiting to speak out about the only thing that is real – Love.

Returning to the true voice occurs after duality dissolves. It occurs when the war with the Self has come to an end, when the need to be seen as something other than *who we really are* dissolves, and when we are certain that not a word is spoken nor an action taken without the Higher Power. Then our doubts and guilt cease, by the Grace of God, and we give up striving to be anything. We are left open and ready for a new foundation to be laid. It is somewhat like the construction of a house; the old structure must be torn down for the new home to be created. When the old conditioned beliefs have become outmoded, ridiculous, and ready to crumble, then, after a time of stillness and nothingness, and settling of dust, we emerge again. Newly reborn, we are filled with the joy of springtime, with a Love that takes over where abandonment once lived. Every day becomes an expression of beauty and the lightness of Love, for we never know what we will do or what will pour out from us. We become a vehicle for the Higher Power, and a pure expression of consciousness. No longer bound by the opinions or rules of the world, our true boss, our true authority, is the voice of our God Self.

✣Meditation Keys – Returning to the True Voice✣

⚿ *Spend some time chanting or speaking out loud whatever name most strongly evokes The Divine – God, Jesus, Allah, Krishna, Shiva, Mohammad, the name of your guru, etc. Do this for about fifteen minutes.*

⚿ *Then sit quietly and observe the voice of your soul emanating from the deep inner silence.*

Dancing in Your Garden

I must have been so blind to have missed you
You have been so close to me,
but I have simply overlooked you
In favor of that which was far from me
Nothing has changed, but everything has changed
For the darkened veil has been removed from my eyes
All the world has become a Garden of Eden
Everything I touch melts into my heart
Everything I see brightens my mind,
like a thousand suns
Everything I taste turns to honey, and all I feel
Is the constant hum of your sweet, still, presence
Dancing in my every cell

When Earth Becomes Heaven

A fter a period of emptying, there comes a time in which every small thing becomes an expression of our God Self. We feel respect for all of life and gratitude for its abundant manifestation. I would watch my Guru, as she approached her chair, bowing to it with the utmost respect before she would sit down. This humble expression of love and humility would always open my heart. In this simple gesture, Gurumayi was bowing to the great Self in herself and in every person and every thing. Nothing needed to be understood but this state of worship that she displayed. Not knowing our true nature, we miss the beauty of the moment because it is either taken for granted, or pushed away to await something better.

This is why we treat each other so poorly; we do not recognize each other as God. Instead of seeing our relationships as Divine blessings for which our heart could
feel grateful, we find fault. We look for others' flaws and
shortcomings, to justify our belief that they are unable
to fulfill our needs. Heaven and earth can never meet as
long as we disrespect and/or hold even one person outside of our heart. This applies to our own Self and to our
environment as well. If there is anywhere that we don't
fully respect the greatness that we are, be it with
friends, relations, money, or possessions, our heart and
our joy will be closed to all that our life presents to us.
As long as we fail to appreciate who we are and what we
have, the door will stay forever closed. Wars will continue, marriages will dissolve, our environment will be
destroyed, and sorrow will continue. We must stop and
approach everything and everyone with Love. We must
bow to our God Self in all of the forms that surround us.
We must thank God every day for the gifts that are here
to support us, for our husband, wife, child, boss, money,
food, or shelter. When we respect everything and we
are grateful for everything, then our world becomes
utterly abundant. We become wealthier than we could
ever imagine. All of our desires are met, all of our
dreams are fulfilled, and our senses are heightened to
finally taste the elixir that has always been available to
us. We become ready to imbibe this nectar only after we
tire of the poisonous drinks of anger, resentment, separation, disrespect, and greed. Instead of looking outside
ourselves for God to come save us, we see that every
moment and every thing we encounter is a Divine
expression. Everything we have ever sought can be
found in every aspect of our life. The great gift of the
purification process is that we gradually become free of

desiring the old ego self, and are ready to accept the Divine key of respect and love for all of life, which opens the door that brings heaven to earth.

✤ Meditation Keys – When Earth Becomes Heaven ✤

🔑 *Look at every moment of life and every possession as a gift to be fully enjoyed with gratitude and respect.*

🔑 *Even disappointment can hold great gifts. If this is your current experience, ask yourself, "What is the gift that this disappointment is offering me?"*

Decoding Darkness

How is it that this beautiful earth
is so filled with pain and darkness?

Who allowed such beauty to be destroyed?
And people to be veiled so completely?

What dark forces of denial programmed us
to look at all that we are not, rather than all that we are?

Who wanted us to be robotic and unquestioning
rather than alive, feeling, and knowing beings?

It's as if a circle of silent denial
has been drawn about us
to make us weak and believe lies.

Someone must be very afraid of the great power that
we all are
to go to so much trouble to hide it from us

Breaking The Code of Delusion

"Believe nothing, no matter where you read it, or who said it, no matter if I have said it, unless it agrees with your own reason and your own common sense."

Buddha

Direct experience is the only Truth. Wisdom arises from direct experience; knowledge arises from accepting someone else's experience or concepts. Power exists within unobstructed self-knowledge in which we directly experience the truth of something. We can tell a child not to put her hands into a fire or she will get burned. If she does it anyway, she will know "first hand" the truth of what happens when she puts her hands into a fire.

When our experiences are not our own, we are subject to manipulation of all kinds. I've observed some healers and teachers practice outright denial and abuse of power. As a result, people are kept down through control, manipulation, self-doubt, and guilt. Because the teacher and his/her organization has a strong energy field, people who are not used to feeling a higher vibration of energy may feel this must be the Truth because their mind is expanded initially. But even the darkest forces on this planet can make people feel more open at first.

I have witnessed a lot of beauty as well as corruption in many spiritual groups. I have met people who have great powers but no humility, and have used these powers to manipulate in order to fulfill their hidden agendas. There are some popular so-called gurus who start out with noble intentions but end up using the spiritual teachings to gain power, control, money, or sex. I have met teachers who have carried their sexual dysfunction into their teachings and have tried, often successfully, to convince their female followers that by sleeping with them they will gain spiritual power. I had a friend who got involved with a quasi-spiritual group in which she was doing some unusual practices that she didn't want to disclose to me. Eventually she ran away from the group because she felt that it was not right to be involved with them. But they had power and an intent to harm others and eventually burned down her apartment.

Having said that, a true Guru's job is no easy task and some followers, whose egos may have been challenged in their learning/purification process, have been known to turn on their guru and try to discredit him or her. So we must deeply trust our intuition and listen to the

Guru that lives inside us. Humility is the key. In all of the years that I have known Gurumayi, she has consistently displayed the utmost humility and respect for life and others. The humility that I have witnessed in meetings with Sant Rajinder Singh always makes me cry as it is so beautiful and pure. There are many wonderful divine beings inhabiting our planet who are models of love and humility and want nothing more than to remind us of our true Self.

If you are in a group that does not have pure intentions, or does not demonstrate ethical behavior, or tries to shame you to keep you under its power, pray with all of your heart for the strength and clarity to know what the absolute Truth is, and to know *who you really are*. But also remember that God comes even in this form, so that we might learn discernment and strengthen our conviction and trust in our own knowing. When someone experiences enlightenment, it is often our concepts of how a liberated being should behave that makes understanding them difficult. They quite likely will retain much of the personality they had prior to their enlightenment experience; the only difference is that they are no longer identified with that personality and therefore do not see themselves as the "doer" of the actions. This is where we need to decide for ourselves whether we can live with a teacher whose behaviour makes us feel uncomfortable. This brings us back to the Oneness in which we must own the situation as another part of us that reflects where we need to bring acceptance, forgiveness and healing to ourselves and to others.

We all desperately need to feel love and we all want to love. But we must be selective and trust that inner voice that always knows the truth. Surrender is never to an outer person or Guru, but to the clear true knowing in our own heart. Gurus and teachers are very important in helping us navigate back to our true Self. They can help pull us out of illusion when we are lost. I could never have found my way without the help of my great teachers. But because we live in bodies with needs and wants, it only makes sense at this time and at this stage in human history, that where there are people there is corruption. In churches, ashrams, mosques, governments, or anywhere that bodies and egos come together, we will find control issues, manipulation, and conflict. When we awaken to our true Self, we can see clearly the maya which has obscured our own knowing. It's as if we've all been mind-controlled to stay down, to stay small, to stay in conflict, self-doubt, and confusion, and to not know *who we really are*. It's as if we have been implanted with unworthiness and guilt so that we will come to understand the consequences of not trusting our own knowing. When we remove the veils from our eyes, we perceive the Truth. When we are established in our real nature, we are no longer controllable for we no longer care to play the game of good/bad, win/lose. It all becomes the same old movie. The old mind and its ways appears ridiculous and uninteresting. We are no longer willing to be overly busy running after the stuff of illusion, and waste valuable time that could be spent merging with our pure Self. The time has come for the purity of our true nature to emerge.

We need to return again to the Source and remember why we came here in the first place. Our deepest visions must be brought forth. Our old fears must be faced and dissolved, freeing us to take the great risks of the heart. Our love is the only thing that will save us. We must give the gift of love to ourselves and to the rest of humanity, despite what criticism may come. The mind is meant to follow the heart, not the other way around. The power of our conditioning has made breaking the code of fear seem too scary. We don't need to concern ourselves about what others, who are still bound, think of our emerging freedom, for everyone has his or her timing, and the true power is Love and not fear. Love cannot be hurt, for it is already free and limitless. Fear is but a mere cloud in the sky of our true nature. Let Love speak with its true voice and let it dissolve the ancient codes of delusion.

The Kiss of Gratitude

Let me gratefully kiss your divine feet...
that spill forth the perfume of the Gods

Let me gratefully kiss this flower, this tree,
this sidewalk...
where love blossoms and love stretches
out to the sun...
and where love walks everyday

Let me gratefully kiss the food...
that this blessed earth has so freely offered to me

Let me gratefully kiss this earth...
and spiral myself in its mud, so I can thank it...
as I swim in its sensuous texture

Let me gratefully kiss this cup...
that is so filled with supreme wealth...
and infinite abundance and gratitude

Let me gratefully kiss and worship your eyes...
that peer out of this miraculous body...
sculpted from Love's hands

How can I thank you...
when the ever-blooming garden of your creation...
is just a manifestation of one continuous thank-you?

True Gratitude

After the cup has emptied and after the darkness, loneliness and abandonment have passed, then the veil is removed to reveal perfect Love. All we can do at this point is say "Thank you." When we realize our true abundance is everything that we are, there is nothing left to do but dance in joy and gratitude. Nothing remains but the constant receiving of blessings. Blessings of God's love permeate every person, every object – everything we see and feel. The joy arises from knowing that I am all of it; I am not separate at all. I am in it and it is in me. Then our soul returns to the Garden of Gratitude forever.

✤Meditation Keys – True Gratitude✤

🔑 *Spend a whole day thanking God for everything you see, everything you do, and everything you hear, feel, and touch.*

To Merge with Your Great Heart

My heart has desired to merge
with your great heart forever
But just when I come close to dissolving in you
My mind becomes very interested
in a piece of your world
And chases after it like a lascivious dog
I wake up the next day and
my arms are empty and cold
And you are gone

My heart has desired to merge
with your great heart forever
But my eyes behold your created beauty and mistake it
for the real thing
As I grasp the empty space, I find nothing but my
desire and lust
Which leaves me bereft and longing for you again

My heart has desired to merge
with your great heart forever
But I have been an unfaithful lover
My need and my greed have pulled me far away from
your love
And yet, I ask you now for your forgiveness
I am on my knees, dried up like a beggar
Having tasted the emptiness
that I have chased for so long

My soul cries out to you – please marry me, please
marry me
Please believe me - I am ready now

My heart has desired to merge
with your great heart forever
My spirit has been strong, but my flesh has been weak
But now even my flesh can no longer turn away from
the Divine door
For it needs and wants only your love
And no other lover will do

My heart has desired to merge
with your great heart forever
And so I lie here, naked and outstretched, awaiting
your response
And the final consummation of your Love
The Love that will end all suffering, all striving,
all illusion
And marry my mind and my heart into
the One Great Heart forever

The Marriage

Long before I even thought of God or spirituality, and when I was very young, I used to whisper inside myself all the time, "Marry me! Marry me!" I had no idea to whom I was speaking. When I grew up, this obsession never left me, even when I did finally marry a man. I could still hear the words, "Marry me! Marry me!"

Later when I had a Guru, I would always know when she passed by, even before I saw her, because the words, "Marry me! Marry me!" would well up so strongly that I wanted to scream them out. I finally realized that my soul was asking to be married or to merge with the Supreme Soul – spirit with form, heart with mind, form with formless. I couldn't bear living in separation, so my whole life became one of divine discontent.

I searched for completion in many ways and in many things and people. But nothing fulfilled me, and my spiritual experiences often felt like a "one night stand," rather than any kind of lasting sense of union. My desire for marriage was of a visceral nature and involved not just my thought processes but my whole body, like a lover needing to merge with his or her beloved partner. The strong physical nature of this need focused me in a way nothing else could. After I projected it on men for a while, I realized the impermanence of human relations, as they would leave me with a profound sense of emptiness. The desire for the marriage ran so deep in me, no man could ever be expected to fulfill it. As I came to this need, I came to terms with my growing disinterest in the outer world. I stopped fighting to be a part of life the way I had once known it and allowed the Divine Lover to draw me in more and more. I was becoming gentle, open, and receptive like a bride who has tossed away her old toys or attachments to any previous loves, in readiness for the true husband. My mind that had once chased and desired the worldly delights was being submerged into the bliss of the Great Heart. Over time, my mind's desires slowly made way for my heart's desires. Then the doors and the barriers between the two became less and less.

✤Meditation Keys – The Marriage✤

Recall a person whom you worship and adore – either now or in the past.

As you think of this person, allow the feeling of longing to arise within you.

Stay with this feeling of longing but take away the face, name, and personality of the person.

Continue to feel this longing inside of yourself and allow it to intensify.

Now redirect this longing toward God as beloved. Even if you don't feel the connection initially, at least you have opened a pathway to express your soul's true desire – to merge back into the Love of God.

Who?

Whose blood runs through these blessed veins?
Who looks out from these blessed eyes?
Who tastes, who feels, who thinks, who touches
through these blessed senses?
Who makes us walk, makes us talk, makes us laugh,
and makes us cry through this blessed body?
All these gifts given freely, just so this WHO we are
seeking can turn our gaze back to the miracle of
the Blessed.

The Blessed

here are so many contradictions and opposing forces in this world that we may well ask, "How can we pull ourselves out of the terrible conflict and judgment of the mind?"

When we feel the need to push one thing or thought away in order to embrace another thing or thought, we create a battle with the ego that can never be won. Our life energy or vibration becomes one of dissonance rather than peace.

Peace begins with us. The gift of the purification process is that we ultimately reach a place where we find that we are incapable of fighting any more. We can no longer engage in the constant inner struggle between the opposing forces of the mind that can never come to resolution. What then is the solution? Peace will only be found when we surrender to That Which is Behind the thoughts, feelings, and struggles. We must always ask, "Who does everything? Who are we really? Who thinks? Who struggles? Who feels? Who are the others who stand before us every day of our life? Who are our children, parents or partners?" When we can look into the eyes of another, we will see that the same soul who lives in us, lives in every living being.

If we see ourselves and each other as blessed, we will be fulfilling the true purpose of our life – God's love. The saints say that nothing that we can do or accomplish in this world will mean anything in the afterlife. The only the thing that matters is Love.

Caroline Myss, a medical intuitive and contemporary spiritual teacher, tells a story about a woman who found herself in a Los Angeles traffic jam. There was a bad car accident some distance down the road, and someone had been seriously hurt. The woman sat in her car and quietly said a prayer in which she blessed the injured person. Many months later, a visitor showed up at her door with flowers. It was the person who had been injured in the accident many months before and had recently come out of hospital. The visitor said that she had had a near death experience after the crash and, after leaving her body, she became acutely aware of the many drivers who were aggravated by the delay caused by the accident. But then she saw a beam of light that uplifted her and she could see this woman praying for her. While still out of her body, the visitor took a mental note of the car's license plate so that she would remember it once she returned to consciousness. She just wanted to acknowledge this woman and thank her for her prayer and blessings. What an incredible example of the true purpose and power of our lives!

If we were to give love and blessings to everyone we meet, there would be no need for war of any kind. Imagine if everyone in the world directed his or her thoughts in this way. Our existence would become one of paradise. If in each moment we could replace our judgments with blessings, conflict would end. Just imagine if we could even bless our enemies. If the whole world joined together to do this supreme practice, we would experience the Oneness that we all are. We would trust each other because we would know that we are held in a place of love. We would forgive each other for any transgressions, as we would be living in a constant state of love. We would feel our worthiness because we would know that we are an integral part of the whole and no matter how ill or aged we might be, our power to bless would be our true service to others and the world.

When our inner war of separating ourselves from the great Love that we already are has come to an end, all that we are left with is the knowledge that we are the Blessing. From a place of Blessing, there can be no high or low, nor any judgment, for all that we see is simply another part of God looking back at us. Only when we realize this viscerally can we truly experience our thoughts as Blessed, our feelings as Blessed, and everyone in our life as Blessed. In fact, all that we see, hear, taste, and smell is Blessed. When we merge with everything that is, we will have found the Magic Doorway into the Divine and we can turn our world into The Blessed.

✤Meditation Keys – The Blessed ✤

Spend the rest of your life affirming every thought, every feeling and every sense experience as Blessed.

Affirm that everywhere you walk and everything you see is Blessed.

See every person in your family and every person you come in contact with as Blessed.

See this entire planet, and all life as Blessed.

Pray that everyone may live a blessed life and share the blessing that they are with everyone in their world.

Room to Be

After the sharp, silver sword of discrimination
Disguised as anger
Stops analyzing and cutting through
All the systems
All the concepts
All the structures and nothing is left
Then there is room for everything to blossom anew
And all of life, as it is,
Has room to be

Dissolving The Last Door To Divinity

Those of us who have watched someone leave this world may experience that person trying to drop whoever they thought they were while inhabiting this world. When my beautiful friend was dying of breast cancer, she struggled with fear, self-judgment, and a sense of incompleteness because of dying at such a young age, right up to the end. But then she finally surrendered completely to what is, and dropped her identification with her body beautifully. Those of us at her bedside knew that she had entered a place of Rapture because the look on her face was ecstatic.

It's at times like these that we see that our lives, problems, and accomplishments are really just mind-generated, and ultimately irrelevant. All that truly matters is how readily we can merge back into the Love of God, the only true Reality.

Stepping out of the labyrinth of the mind dissolves the last door to Divinity. Looking over my manuscript for this book, I became aware of the contradictions, opinions, and concepts in my written commentary. I saw how the mind contradicts itself. One day it feels strongly about one thing and the next day it no longer cares, as it is on to something else. It's like trying to make up nothing from nothing. By the end of the book I no longer believed anything I was writing. Everything I tried to conceptualize dissolved into thin air, leaving nothing but a void of stillness in its wake. Each chapter was emptying more and more from me, until that which was real became stronger than the unreal and the temporary. However, after I finished writing this book, a great doubt arose and I questioned myself, "Who am I to be writing a spiritual book with all of my weird idiosyncrasies and insecurities?" Then the next morning, while I was doing weights at the gym, I was struck with the absolute understanding that I did not write this book. I felt such freedom, joy, and gratitude to the One Who Does All Actions, for freeing me from my ego that would have me believe that I am the doer of any action – especially writing this book. My ego had previously been carrying the load of bringing this book to fruition, like an interminable pregnancy. After a long and arduous birthing period, I felt the same attachment to this book as a mother feels at the birth of her child. But when I was shown who had been writing it all along, I no longer worried about its content or outcome as I knew something much greater than my small ego self knew what it wanted to say and for whom it wanted to say it. My idiosyncrasies and insecurities are God-given to create this unique vehicle in the form of Devrah, through which this book could come forth. So when

I dropped the ego concept of being the writer of this book, all that was left was the moment. There was nothing more to say and nothing more to do. Something had indeed changed and something was being birthed, but it wasn't just this book. All that I felt was love, all that I saw was love, and all that I heard was love. When the mind's made-up worlds finally fall to rest, the last door to Divinity dissolves.

✦ Meditation Keys –
Dissolving the Last Door to Divinity ✦

Spend some time letting everything drop away from you – any ideas you have about yourself, any aches or pains, worries, thoughts, fears or any concept at all about anything. See all of this melting off your body.

Sit with what is left. Feel the breath loving you as it enters your body, and loving you as it leaves your body.

Feel the breath bringing you closer to the pure and empty state, the space between thoughts or breaths, for this is where God dwells.

The Birth

Then the Being from the far away galaxy looked down upon the earth, and to her great surprise saw beautiful pastel colors circling the atmosphere. An aroma of Divine flower-like essences emanated from Earth to the whole Universe. As she looked through the soft haze that surrounded the globe, she saw the same people who were previously tortured and in pain, dancing and spiraling in states of supreme joy and ecstasy. All bondage had dissolved, all fear, all pain. Great fresh, clear bubbling waters and exquisitely colored landscapes replaced the smoky, dirty, brown polluted areas. A golden pink light radiated out from every mountaintop. Perplexed by this miraculous transformation, the Being again asked God, "What happened? How did this planet evolve from such darkness into such light? And how did all the people become so joyous?"

God replied: "It's only Love that creates such beauty, for without Love, all is darkness, evil, pollution, and insurmountable grief. There comes a time when the sadness and corruption become so great that I must intervene and renovate the old to make room for the new. When the heaviness is just about to destroy earth, I plant a few souls on the planet to sing the song of Love. As the song is sung, many hear it and join together to sing. And as this prayer of Love becomes stronger, the renewal takes place. That which cannot stand in this pure vibration is cleansed away. Doors, which have been slammed shut for centuries, are ripped from their frames. Old structures dissolve and anything that has blocked the open door of Love and pure consciousness is ushered out. This divine song of Love enters into the cells of everyone, and creates a rejuvenation unlike anything that has ever been witnessed in this entire Universe. So we have the great power of the human spirit, and as you have seen, there is no greater power than the power of Love. When millions gather together in my name, and all the closed doors of the heart are open, everything is possible.

Thou art the heavens, and Thou art the earth:
Thou alone art day and night and air:
Thou Thyself art all things that have birth,
Even the offerings of flowers fair.

Lalleshwari

I have fallen in love, O Mother,
With the beautiful One who knows no birth
And knows no fear.

Akka Mahadevi

Notes

1. Matthew 5:44 to 48, *The Holy Bible*, King James Version.

2. Enlightenment is a term for the realization of the very core of all that is eternal, free of all concepts; it is the Reality that lies beyond the mind.

3. Jaideva Singh, *Spanda Karikas*. Delhi: Motilal Banarsidass, 1980, inside front of book cover.

4. Transmutation means using everything we experience to enter into pure awareness.

5. Jaideva Singh, Op. Cit., p. 104.

6. Kahlil Gibran, *The Prophet*. New York: Alfred A. Knopf, 1989, p. 13.

7. Sams, Jamie and Carson, David. *Medicine Cards*. Santa Fe: Bear & Company, p. 61.

8. Kahlil Gibran, Op. Cit., p. 12.

9. Kahlil Gibran, Op. Cit., p. 13.

10. Rajinder Singh, *Empowering Your Soul Through Meditation*. Boston: Element, 1999, p. 98.

11. Raj Kumar Bagga, *The Anurag Sagar of Kabir*. Sanbornton, New Hampshire: Sant Bani Ashram, 1995. Prologue, pg. xxvii.

12. Raj Kumar Bagga, Op. Cit., p. 7.

13. Rajinder Sing, Op. Cit., Pg. 99.

14. Swami Muktananda, "The Ego and Beyond," *Darshan* Magazine #44. New York: SYDA Foundation, pg. 34.

15. *Vijnanabhairava or Divine Consciousness*, translated by Jaideva Singh. Delhi: Motilal Banarsidass, 1979, Dharana # 75.

16. Swami Anantananda, *What's On My Mind?* New York: SYDA Foundation, 1996, p. 65.

17. Swami Muktananda, *I Have Become Alive*. New York: SYDA Foundation, 1985, p. 160-61.

18. Quoted by Swami Anantananda, Op. Cit., p. 74.

19. Quoted by Douglas Keller, "Thieves of the Heart," *Darshan* Magazine #50. New York: SYDA Foundation, p. 22.

20. Gurumayi Chidvilasananda, *Darshan* Magazine #50. New York: SYDA Foundation, pg. 11-12

21. Sogyal Rinpoche, *The Tibetan Book of Living and Dying*. San Francisco: HarperCollins Publishers, p. 123.

22. Ramesh Balsekar, *Your Head in the Tiger's Mouth*. California: Advaita Press, 1988, p. 253-254

23. Sogyal Rinpoche, Op. Cit., p. 114.

24. *A Course in Miracles*. California: Foundation for Inner Peace, 1975-85, Chapter 1, Verse 7, p. 1.

25. Quoted in *The Odyssey of Enlightenment* by Berthold Madhukar Thompson. California: Wisdom Editions, 2003, page 252.

26. Sant Darshan Singh, *Spiritual Awakening*. India: Sawan Kirpal Publications, 1981, p. 246.

27. Evelyn Underhill, *Mysticism*. New York: New American Library, 1974, p. 412.

28. Quoted in *Mysticism* by Evelyn Underhill, p. 392.

29. Quoted in *Mysticism* by Evelyn Underhill, p. 389.

30. Quoted in *Mysticism* by Evelyn Underhill, p. 399.

31. Quoted in *Mysticism* by Evelyn Underhill, p. 390.

32. *Women Saints East and West*. Ed. By Swami Ghanananda and Sir John Stewart-Wallace. Hollywood: Vedanta Press, p. 55.

33. Quoted in *Mysticism* by Evelyn Underhill, p. 421.

34. Gurumayi Chidvilasananda, *My Lord Loves A Pure Heart*. New York: SYDA Foundation, 1994, p.20

35. Attributed to Jesus in the Gospel of Thomas (Gnostic).

36. Quoted from the website, http://www.askgrace.com.

ISBN 978-0-9784986-0-3